MW00946348

My Friend Joe:
Reflections on St. Joseph

Susan Rose Francois, CSJP

Susan Rose Francois, CSJP is Assistant Congregation Leader of the Congregation of the Sisters of St. Joseph of Peace. She writes regularly for *Global Sisters Report* on religious life, social justice, and spirituality. Her personal blog, *At the Corner of St. Joseph*, can be found at susanandstjoseph.com. Sister Susan was a Bernardin Scholar at Catholic Theological Union where she earned her MA in theology.

My Friend Joe:
Reflections on St. Joseph

Susan Rose Francois, CSJP

Kenmare Press
2021

Copyright © 2021 by Sisters of St. Joseph of Peace

All rights reserved. This book or any portion thereof may not be reproduced or used in any manner whatsoever without the express written permission of the publisher except for the use of brief quotations in a book review or scholarly journal.

Scripture texts in this work are taken from the *New American Bible, revised edition* © 2010, 1991, 1986, 1970 Confraternity of Christian Doctrine, Washington, D.C. and are used by permission of the copyright owner. All Rights Reserved. No part of the New American Bible may be reproduced in any form without permission in writing from the copyright owner.

First Printing: 2021

ISBN: 978-1-105-71197-8
eISBN: 978-1-304-35402-0

Library of Congress Control Number: 2021915785

Kenmare Press
399 Hudson Terrace
Englewood Cliffs, NJ 07632
www.csjp.org/kenmarepress

Contents

I dedicate this little book of reflections
on St. Joseph to ...

My parents,
Eileen Mary Schmelzer Francois
and Francis Bernard Francois,
for the gift of life and everything else.

My religious community,
the Sisters of St. Joseph of Peace,
for encouraging,
challenging,
and sustaining
me on the journey
to pursue social justice
as a path to peace.

My spiritual friend,
Margaret Anna Cusack,
known in religion as Mother Francis Clare,
known to me simply as MAC,
for sharing her gift of writing and for
inspiring me to do the same.

And of course, St. Joseph himself,
my friend Joe,
for his steady presence,
model of peace,
and spiritual friendship.

List of Photographs

All photographs were taken by the author. Each picture provides a different perspective on St. Joseph which inspired the author's reflection included in that Chapter. Digital copies of the photographs are available on the author's blog to be downloaded for personal use, At the Corner of Susan and St. Joseph, susanandstjoseph.com/my-friend-joe.

Cover

St. Joseph watching the forest at St. Mary-on-the-Lake, Bellevue, Washington. May 19, 2019

Introduction

Statue of St. Joseph, with flowers, in the corner of the chapel at the CSJP house on Walm Lane, London, England. July 6, 2018.

Chapter 1 – Joseph Never Fails

Small statue of St. Joseph with ceramic container in the front parlor of Mater Dei Convent, Englewood Cliffs, New Jersey. July 16, 2020.

Chapter 2 – The Unexpected

Stained-glass window behind the altar at St. Joseph Chapel, St. Joseph Village, Chicago, Illinois. January 26, 2020.

Chapter 3 – Present of Presence

Statue of St. Joseph overlooking an evergreen tree, which is adorned with decorative Christmas lights, outside Bon Secours Retreat and Conference Center, Marriottsville, Maryland. November 18, 2018.

Chapter 4 – Rise and Take Up the Child

Marble wall relief of the Holy Family's Flight to Egypt, St. Hugh's Catholic Church, Lincoln, England. February 12, 2019.

Chapter 5 – Limitless Family

Statue of St. Joseph and Jesus in front of AMITA Health St. Joseph Hospital, on the shores of Lake Michigan in Chicago, Illinois. November 19, 2017.

Chapter 6 – Watching the Workers

Statue of St. Joseph the Worker with a carpenter's van parked in the background, outside Holy Name Medical Center, Teaneck, New Jersey. January 11, 2019.

Chapter 7 – A Happy Life

Wooden statute of St. Joseph from the American Southwest, taken in the room of Sister Susan Dewitt at Gaffney Hall, St. Mary-on-the-Lake, Bellevue, Washington. March 1, 2019.

Conclusion – Your Friend Joe

Budding springtime flowers with St. Joseph statue in the background, outside St. Michael Villa, Englewood Cliffs, New Jersey. July 1, 2020.

Appendix II

Prayer space featuring the icon of St. Joseph of Peace, taken at the CSJP Autumn Assembly held at the Peace and Spirituality Center, Bellevue, Washington. November 3, 2018.

St. Joseph sleeping on a bed of prayer requests in the author's personal prayer space in Mater Dei convent, Englewood Cliffs, New Jersey. November 14, 2020.

Introduction

THIS BOOK is a work of prayer. Prayer to and with St. Joseph has fostered my own relationship with him over the years, especially since I entered the Sisters of St. Joseph of Peace. More than 15 years later, I consider him a spiritual friend, one I affectionately call "My Friend Joe."

Another of my spiritual friends, Margaret Anna Cusack, known in religion as Mother Francis Clare, chose St. Joseph as the patron for her new community because she considered him to be a model of peace. "No doubt we may point to St. Joseph as the great model of every virtue, but it would seem as if peace was his crowning grace."[1]

The Constitutions of the Sisters of St. Joseph of Peace expand on this tradition.

> From the beginning of the congregation
> Joseph was chosen as our patron
> because he is a model of peace.
> His courage to live a life of faith
> inspires us to trust in God's abiding love,
> especially in times of struggle and uncertainty.
>   (Constitution 36)

Surely we, each of us, need friends who can help us to trust in God's abiding love during challenging times. We live in times of struggle and uncertainty on a grand and fast-moving scale. I don't know about you, but sometimes I find myself simply weary amid the chaos of life today.

My friendship with St. Joseph has been an anchor in the storm. He provides the kind of listening ear you only find in

---

[1] Margaret Anna Cusack (Mother Clare), "St. Joseph's Confraternity of Peace," 1883, quoted in Joan Ward, CSJP and Catherine O'Connor, CSJP, *A Great Love of Peace: Insights into the Charism and Spirituality of the Sisters of St. Joseph of Peace* (self-pub., 2000), 9.

someone who has journeyed through their own stormy weather and come out on the other side, trusting even more in God's faithful love.

St. Joseph is not only the patron of our Congregation, we are also named after him. I have a fondness for the original construction of our moniker—St. Joseph's Sisters of Peace. There is inherent relationship, connection, and daughterliness embodied in this original name.

Mother Clare's prayer, that the "very name, Sisters of Peace, will, it is hoped, inspire the desire of peace and a love for it," is recorded in our original 1884 Constitutions. This has certainly been true in my life as a vowed member of the Congregation. After all, it was the charism of pursuing peace through justice that led me to the community in the first place.

The word "peace" was removed from our name in 1929, not because it was not desired as a virtue, but rather because the name "Sisters of Peace" was associated with our controversial founder, Mother Clare. Two years before I was born, at the General Chapter in 1970, peace was returned to our name as a result of the sisters' faithful response to the Second Vatican Council, also reuniting us with Mother Clare.[2] For this I am very grateful.

I am also grateful that St. Joseph was always with us in our name, our faithful friend. When we were St. Joseph's Sisters of Peace, he was our model of that virtue. When we were the Sisters of St. Joseph of Newark, the name chosen by the Vatican in 1929 because our motherhouse was located in that diocese, St. Joseph safeguarded this virtue for us to find

---

[2] Susan Dewitt, "History and Roots: Reclaiming Peace," *Living Peace,* Winter 2014, 20. For more of the story of Mother Clare, see Dorothy Vidulich's *Peace Pays a Price: A Study of Margaret Anna Cusack,* also published by Kenmare Press.

in his life story and in our own hearts and lives, if not in our name.

My desire for peace, and a love for it, drew me to the Congregation. This has only grown. So too has my desire for spiritual friendship with St. Joseph, and a love for him, grown within me, inspired by our present name, the Sisters of St. Joseph of Peace.

The photo at the beginning of this introduction is from the chapel at our house on Walm Lane in London. I was lucky enough to spend part of my apostolic novitiate year with our sisters in the United Kingdom. I worked with men and women experiencing homelessness on the streets of London, making them tea and toast and helping them to look for work. When I came home, I would pop into the chapel to pray with St. Joseph and share my care and concern for the people I'd met that day, as well as prayers for my own vocational discernment. St. Joseph listened quite a bit to me in the three short months I lived at Walm Lane. Looking back, I think praying with St. Joseph in that chapel was the beginning of our friendship. Whenever I return to Walm Lane to visit our sisters, I always make sure to check in with my friend Joe and admire the flowers our sisters have placed before him. I would guess that he is their friend too.

* * *

This book is a work of memory. My own memories—of family life, ministry, and world events—are intertwined with the Church's memory of St. Joseph—his family life, work, and the political events swirling around the infant Jesus.

You will not find an in-depth history or analysis of St. Joseph in this little book of reflections. In part this is because we know so little about St. Joseph, either as an historical figure or as recorded in scripture. Much of what we understand about Joseph comes to us from tradition and the lived experience of the faithful over the centuries.

A few years ago, looking for a gift for one of my religious sisters, I stumbled upon a website that sells religious socks. Yes, that's right, you too can adorn your feet with images of saints with a famous quote from the saint printed on the sole of the sock. I bought two pairs of the St. Joseph socks, one for my friend and one for myself. I couldn't resist. When I first put on my pair, my eyes were drawn to the sole. Where the words of St. Joseph should be, there were simply empty quotation marks. I remember laughing out loud. Joseph must have said something over his life, but of course none of his words are recorded in scripture.

Scripture does tell us, however, that he was a just man who more than once responded to the message of an angel. We remember that he was the loving spouse of Mary and foster father of Jesus. We remember him as a carpenter and as a quiet, humble, and virtuous man. Each of these memories is embodied in the tradition and teaching on Joseph.

In researching this tradition, I discovered a few things. I learned that Pope Leo XIII—the same pontiff that met with Mother Clare and approved our Congregation—not only wrote *Rerum Novarum*, the first major encyclical of Catholic Social Thought, but also an encyclical on St. Joseph, *Quamquam Pluries.* I learned that Pope John XXIII declared St. Joseph to be the patron saint of the Second Vatican Council, the same Council that led my Congregation to reclaim our name and our founder. I began to understand how the memory of St. Joseph persisted, while a love and devotion to him grew in the hearts of the faithful. As often happens, it took a little while for the institutional church to catch up.

* * *

This book is a work of imagination. Given that so little is actually known about the historical figure of St. Joseph, or recorded in scripture, much if not most of our traditions come from the hearts and imaginations of the faithful. Family is central to his story. Family is central to our story. In the tradition around St. Joseph, our families of all shapes and sizes meet.

The idea for this book first came to me through photography. Each reflection, in fact, was inspired by a photo I took of St. Joseph, or rather, a photo of an artist's imaginative rendering of him.

Once you start looking for St. Joseph in art and sculpture, you'll discover that he's hard to find. There's a reason for this. Joseph did not even begin to appear in religious art until the beginning of the Byzantine epoch and the High Middle Ages.[3] When he was depicted, it was often on the margins of the nativity scene, as a spectator or hanger-on rather than as a major figure in his own right. Art devoted to Joseph grew as the faithful's imagination and understanding of Joseph developed over time.

If you keep an eye out, however, you can find St. Joseph, most often depicted in statues located near churches, convents, retreat centers, and hospitals. As I have looked for Joseph, my imagination has been sparked not only by the statue or image, but by his surroundings, the world around him. These scenes have inspired my reflections in this book, imagining how St. Joseph relates with us, advocates for us, and prays for us now through the interplay of his image and the story of life and faith taking place among us today.

* * *

This book is a work of love. You will read in this book not only about my love for St. Joseph, but also for my family, friends, community, church, people marginalized by society, and our wider world. My friend Joe helps me to make sense of it all, to hold the concerns of the world in my heart, and to

---

[3] See *St. Joseph in Art: Iconology and Iconography of the Redeemer's silent Guardian* by Sandro Barbagallo for a thorough analysis of artists imagining and imaging St. Joseph.

turn to him when it might just be a bit too much. St. Joseph, patron of my religious community and patron of the universal church, watches over us and protects us. He also happens to be very good at helping us to get out of sticky situations.

Pope Francis, too, has a spiritual friendship with St. Joseph, a "person whom I love very much, someone who is, and has been, very important throughout my life."[4] He is reported to have discovered his vocation while praying in the Church of St. Joseph in Buenos Aires at the age of 17. Jorge Mario Bergolio became Pope Francis on the Feast of St. Joseph in 2013.

In his personal study in Rome, Pope Francis has a statue of St. Joseph sleeping. Joseph of course received messages from the angels when he was asleep, and his human action made the dream a reality, marrying and forming a family with Mary, and then leading the Holy Family to safety in Egypt. Pope Francis has an imaginative prayer practice that I myself have adopted. He writes down his biggest problems and worries on slips of paper, slides the paper under the statue of the sleeping Joseph, and trusts him to take care of the problem.[5]

"He is the one I go to," Pope Francis told a group of men and women experiencing homelessness in Washington, D.C., "whenever I am 'in a fix.' You make me think of St. Joseph. Your faces remind me of his." He went on to draw a connection between the hardships Joseph faced in his life—with faith and courage—and their own difficulties.

---

[4] Pope Francis, *Visit to the Charitable Center of St. Patrick Parish and Meeting with the Homeless,* September 24, 2015, Vatican.va.

[5] Gelsomino Del Guercio, "Why is Pope Francis so devoted to St. Joseph Sleeping and to the Virgin Mary, Untier of Knots?," Church, *Aleteia,* May 2, 2018, http://aleteia.org/2018/05/02/why-is-pope-francis-so-devoted-to-st-joseph-asleep-and-to-the-virgin-mary-untier-of-knots/. See Appendix II for a prayer service for the Feast of St. Joseph that incorporates this practice.

Introduction

As Pope Francis so deftly illustrates, Joseph is relatable. While we tend to think of him as a father figure and protector, in my experience he is also a friend. He is a special friend who is with you wherever you go, in good times and in bad. "Each of us can discover in Joseph—the man who goes unnoticed, a daily, discreet and hidden presence—an intercessor, a support and a guide in times of trouble."[6]

I invite you to meet my friend Joe. You will find in the chapters that follow my own reflections on St. Joseph. The pictures that inspired them each speak to a different aspect of St. Joseph. I have also included a bit from the tradition of the Church about that face, or perspective, of St. Joseph. Finally, each section ends with two prayers, one from the tradition and one written by me.

My hope is that this book will help you to discover, or deepen, your own spiritual friendship with St. Joseph. You may want to read the book all at one time. You may wish to reflect with one particular chapter. It could be that you too are drawn to one of the pictures and choose to read that section first. How you read this book is up to you. As you read these pages, my prayer is simply that you go to Joseph, and that you go in peace.

---

[6] Pope Francis, *Patris Corde: Apostolic Letter on the 150th Anniversary of the Proclamation of Saint Joseph as Patron of the Universal Church*, December 8, 2020, Vatican.va.

Chapter 1: Joseph Never Fails

"St. Joseph never fails. He always answers petitions."
~ Dorothy Day

IT CAN be easy to feel weighed down by the concerns of the world.

Our daily lives and relationships are sometimes fraught with tension or daunting circumstance, leading us to worry and become weary under the weight of it all. Throw into the mix the various responsibilities of family, work, and community, spiced with the geopolitical and social context of our day, and let's just say there are a lot of petitions filling our hearts and minds. I know my own are filled to the brim on any given day.

Enter St. Joseph, ready to help us carry the load and intercede for us. We need only ask.

Dorothy Day used to picket St. Joseph, praying for his intercession. Not enough money to pay the rent or buy food for the hungry? She'd invite her Catholic Worker community to join her in picketing St. Joseph. Her faith in and love of him grew, especially when time and again, after petitioning Joseph, the exact sum of money needed for the ministry would be provided through one source or another. She described this prayer practice in a 1936 column.

> We picketed St. Joseph this past month, when we were sending out the appeal—asking him to take care of our temporal necessities ... It was a peaceful and loving picketing, the crowd of us taking turns to go to the church and there in the presence of Christ our Leader, contemplate St. Joseph, that great friend of God and Protector of His Church. One of the girls in St. Joseph's house, when we announced the picketing

at the breakfast table, wanted to know, very startled, whether she would have to carry a sign.[7]

I love that image, carrying a sign in the chapel while picketing Joe, drawing his attention and pleading for his intercession. Of course, no signs were involved, other than the ones written on the hearts of those who took their prayers to Joseph on behalf of the community.

Decades later, in a 1956 column, Dorothy reflected: "St. Joseph never fails. He always answers petitions." Experience told her so. She believed "it was St. Joseph who provided the wherewithal to keep our House of Hospitality and *Catholic Worker* headquarters going."[8]

I imagine that St. Joseph holds it all in his own heart. Like his faithful companion Mary, he ponders the concerns of his family and prays for us all, especially the most desperate cases among us.

One day, during the shelter in-place-orders of the coronavirus pandemic, like many people I was working from home. The day in question had been filled with endless video conference meetings, covering this topic and that, all urgent and important with constantly shifting dynamics. Every day seemed to be like that, truth be told. The weight of the world was becoming a bit too much. I was weary. I was worried. I wasn't feeling quite up to the tasks entrusted to me.

Then out of the corner of my eye I spotted this statue of St. Joseph on a side table in our front parlor, peering into the ceramic container by his side. I imagined this is where he keeps all the petitions sent to him when it gets to be too much even for him; a place to hold them lovingly and reverently, making sure not to lose track of anything on his prayer to-do list. He'd of course have made the container out of wood, given

---

[7] Dorothy Day, Day after Day, *Catholic Worker*, October 1936, 4.
[8] Dorothy Day, "May Day," *Catholic Worker,* May 1956, 2.

his chosen profession, but this blue petition container matched his outfit so nicely. I stayed with the image, humoring my prayerful imagination. I was drawn to document the scene with a photo. The caption that came to me was "Joseph ponders the needs of the world," along with this poem.

So here is Joseph,
who never fails.
Standing tall,
but barely taller than the needs of the world.
Looking tenderly
upon our cares and concerns,
the needs of the family of God,
his family,
us.

I found this experience oddly comforting that day. The reflection replenished my resources, renewed my spirits, and helped me to return to my own overflowing to-do list, knowing that I was never alone. My friend Joe was with me, helping to carry the load and seeing what he could do to lighten it. He does have some quite powerful connections after all.

From the Tradition

Margaret Anna Cusack, known in religion as Mother Francis Clare, included a hymn praising St. Joseph's faithful and powerful response to prayer in her 1881 collection of hymns and songs for children.[9]

Holy Joseph, dearest father,
To thy children's prayer incline,
Whilst we sing thy joys and sorrows,
And the glories which are thine.

---

[9] Mary Francis Clare Cusack, *Cloister Songs and Hymns for Children* (London: Burns and Co., 1881), 43.

How to praise thee, how to thank thee,
Blessed saint, we cannot tell;
Favours countless thou hast given—
Can we chose but love thee well?

Her commentary below the hymn notes that the "hymn was written for a community of Poor Clares who received some very special favours through the intercession of St. Joseph." Three years later, after her own departure from the Poor Clare community and subsequent decision to begin a new order, the Sisters of Peace, she would choose St. Joseph as the patron for the new community. She must have known the power of his intercession in her own life.

Just over a decade earlier, the 1870 decree issued by the Sacred Congregation of Rites under Pope Pius IX, elevating the feast of St. Joseph, acknowledged not only his place of honor in the Church, but that the church "has besought his intercession in times of trouble."[10] While today's readers may be surprised 150 years later, the ecclesial and social context of the time was described in the document as "most troublesome ... weighed down by calamities so heavy."

It was within this context of trouble and calamity that petitions were sent to Pius IX from his brother Bishops and the faithful the world over. They prayed "that he would deign to constitute St. Joseph Patron of the Church." This desire for the formal protection of St. Joseph had been a deep desire expressed at the First Ecumenical Council of the Vatican which had just concluded.

The Church's love of and faith in the prayer of St. Joseph had been growing gradually over time.[11] The silence of early Christians about Joseph echoed his silenced words,

---

[10] Sacred Congregation of Rites, *Quemadmodum Deus*, December 8, 1870. http://osjusa.org/st-joseph/magisterium/quemadmodum-deus/

[11] See Appendix I for a chronology of the Church's growing relationship with St. Joseph.

unrecorded in the Gospels. His feast on March 19th was not entered into the *Breviary* or *Roman Missal* until 1479, under Pope Sixtus IV. Joseph was missing or relegated to the background of religious art for centuries, only beginning to gain prominence in iconography in the Byzantine era and High Middle Ages. His name did not even appear in martyrologies and calendars until the ninth century.

For centuries, Joseph waited patiently in the wings, as it were, ready to listen to our prayers, spoken and unspoken. He silently watched over and protected us, just as he was the guardian of his own family. Over time, his wider family came to rely on his prayer and intercession in their lives.

The people of God increasingly knew they could seek the intercession of St. Joseph, and that he would answer. In 1556, St. Joseph was chosen as protector of the city of Puebla in Mexico, as patron of rainstorms and lightening, both of which the city often faced. After the city survived storms in 1611 and 1637, the people prayed in gratitude to St. Joseph, who had not failed them, with mass and a novena.[12]

In the sixteenth century, Teresa of Ávila—the holy woman later declared a saint herself, as well as the first woman named a Doctor of the Church—experienced firsthand the power of St. Joseph's intercessions. As a young girl suffering from paralysis, she took St. Joseph as her personal advocate. "I took for my advocate and lord the glorious Saint Joseph and commended myself earnestly to him," she wrote in her autobiography. She was healed. "I do not remember even now that I have ever asked anything of him which he has failed to grant."[13]

---

[12] Charlene Villaseñor Black, *Creating the Cult of St. Joseph: Art and Gender in the Spanish Empire* (Princeton, NJ: Princeton University Press, 2006, 31.

[13] Teresa of Ávila, *The Life of Teresa of Jesus: The Autobiography of Teresa of Ávila*, trans. E. Allison Peers (New York: Image Books, 1991), http://www.carmelitemonks.org/Vocation/teresa_life.pdf, 51-2.

Over time, personal and collective human experience has influenced magisterial tradition. Petitions to Joseph himself led to petitions to the Pope and First Vatican Council on his behalf. Fitting, really, if you stop and think about it, picketing the Church for Joe.

From the Manual of Prayers for the Sisters of St. Joseph of Newark, 1961

O most faithful guardian on earth of heavenly treasures, my most loving father and advocate, St. Joseph, I have devout recourse to thee, seeing the riches and splendor of the high gifts and favors thou has received in heaven. I recommend to thee with full and open heart this affair which is before me and makes me so anxious. Obtain for me, O great Saint and blessed father, this favor which I implore, in memory of the ineffable glory into which thou wast taken by the Blessed Trinity as soon as heaven was opened to thee by Jesus. Present me before the most merciful throne of God, and say: "O Blessed Trinity, pity this poor creature for the humble reverence and love I bore toward Thee on earth, and for the sublime degree of glory with which it has pleased Thee, to honor me in heaven." Our Father. Hail Mary. Glory Be.

Prayer to St. Joseph, Who Never Fails

St Joseph, we share our prayers and petitions with you, knowing that you are always paying attention, ready to help craft a solution.

Patient and present, you answered the call of an angel that made no earthly sense. You stood by Mary. You raised Jesus. Your words are not recorded, but your actions speak volumes. We come to you often, our steady friend, you who never fail nor tire of our petitions. And here I come, once again, to ask for your intercession [share your worries with St. Joseph].

Amen

Chapter 2: The Unexpected

"It is a very precise moment, that of 'being raised from sleep,' in which St. Joseph, ... is transformed ..."
~ Sandro Barbagallo

WHAT WOULD you do if an angel appeared to you in a dream and told you something completely unexpected, life changing, and a little bit crazy?

In my life, I've certainly not had any mystical experiences involving angels or any other celestially delivered message. Nevertheless, I'd be lying to myself if I didn't acknowledge that, somehow, despite all my protective armor, God has managed to break through, surprising me time and again with the unexpected. More than once, it has been through the message not of an angel, but of a friend.

While I was raised in a good Catholic family and attended Catholic school for 12 years, God and I have had a topsy-turvy relationship over the years, at least on my end. God was always faithful, ever patient, and super persistent, I realize now. Me, on the other hand, well, let's just say that as a young adult I took a twelve-year break from the active practice of my faith.

Looking back, I never really stopped believing in God. I had a lot of questions, however, mostly centered on the existence of suffering. Then there was the problematic reality of human institutions. It was during this time that the dual crises of sexual abuse and abuse of power in the church came into the spotlight, making it that much easier to stay away.

I learned a lot about myself and my role in the world during those years away from the Church. I was drawn to service, and after college I began working in local government, committed to making a difference. In my free time, I volunteered with a variety of good organizations that helped the poor and marginalized. Soon, my job became the career I had always wanted. I had a great group of friends. Life was mostly going in expected directions in my mid-to-late twenties, which was good. And yet, something was missing.

Telling this story now, my forty-nine-year-old self is so very grateful that my twenty-five-year-old self decided to take the leap and explore the question of what was missing in psychotherapy. Self-awareness is a life-long project, but I am certainly more forgiving of myself and others now than I was in my twenties. The biggest gift, and surprise, of this inner work was coming to understand that not only am I worthy of love, I am indeed God's beloved. In my experience, that is the real crisis in our world today. Too many people do not really know and believe in their hearts that they are beloved children of God. We certainly do not act as if we understand this truth, or that this also applies to everyone else. But I digress.

One unexpected result of this time in my life is that I became drawn to seek quiet spaces where I could sit and reflect. Remember, my relationship with God was complicated, so I didn't call it prayer. First, I became a member of a local Japanese garden and found such peace there in the early morning or late afternoon, before or after the crowds. The light of God's love was peeking through the leaves of the trees, right into my own heart. Slowly, but surely, I began to feel the call to find a community to reflect with. There was a local Friends Meeting House near where I lived which a coworker attended, and I went there a few times, testing the waters. I was seeking quiet, I was seeking community, I began to wonder if I was seeking God, but it was not a fit for this ex-Catholic.

God broke through my armor again, this time through my college friend Kimberlee Stafford who invited me to her Catholic parish to support her as she was installed on the

Pastoral Council. I went. I will never forget the feeling, sitting in the pew that day. God's love was so clear and present to me; it brought unexpected tears to my eyes. It was almost like a celestial message from the heavens, although it certainly took me a while to really hear it and accept the invitation. The next Sunday, I woke up and decided I wanted to go to Church again, but I told myself (and God) quite emphatically, this by no means meant I was Catholic again. The next week was the same. This went on for a couple of months until, to make a long story shorter, I not only became Catholic again but my call to service began to make sense. I shifted my volunteer gigs to my parish—Sunday School teacher for the little ones, sponsor for a woman entering the church, food pantry, peace and justice commission, young adult group, pastoral council... You can see the writing on the wall, can't you?

Once again, however, I was not able to hear the call clearly on my own. It took my friend and pastor, Father Steve Bossi, CSP, asking me *the* question—pointing out that perhaps I was being called to use my gifts in the service of my faith— before I really began to explore a religious vocation. The idea had been percolating somewhere below the surface, ever since those early days back in the Church, especially in the quiet moments. I was very adept, however, at ignoring it or pushing the idea away as completely bonkers. Me, a nun? Did people still do that? Then, after a spirit-filled Easter, Father Steve asked me the question. My heart stopped. I knew I had to explore the possibility. The rest is history, or at least my story in the making.

I wonder, is that how Joseph felt when he woke up from his dream? Did his heart stop for a beat or two as he absorbed the unexpected news of Mary's pregnancy and what it meant for his life's journey and purpose?

Maybe that's why I love the stained-glass window pictured at the beginning of this chapter so much. You see this window when you face the altar in the Chapel of St. Joseph at St.

Joseph Village, the nursing home on the North Side of Chicago where my Dad lived his last years. St. Joseph Village was the first ministry of the Franciscan Sisters of Chicago, founded in 1897. The current building is a new construction, and it is clear that special attention was given to the design of the chapel. It is a beautiful place to pray, filled with light.

Joseph does not respond to the angel's heavenly message with words, at least not according to Matthew's Gospel account (2: 18-25). This stained-glass window, however, implies what must have been his natural response. "His expression," notes the booklet describing the chapel artwork, "seems to suggest the question, 'What does this mean?'"[14]

Not only does his expression speak volumes, but also Joseph's posture—hands open, shoulders shrugged, one knee on the ground. He has even dropped his tools. His life will never be the same.

The angel tells Joseph not to be afraid to welcome Mary into his home, to form a family. "For it is through the Holy Spirit that this child has been conceived in her." Joseph, a man of few words—or no words at least that have been recorded—spoke instead with his actions. Joseph was open to the unexpected. Joseph took Mary into his home and helped to raise Jesus. "Joseph's ordinary life of labor and purity of intention have been transformed into an extraordinary element of God's holy plan."[15]

From the Tradition

Sandro Barbagallo, Curator of the Department of Historical Collections for the Vatican Museums, observes that artists have portrayed this pivotal moment in the Christian story "very rarely indeed." Yet this is the scene, and the

---

[14] Franciscan Communities. "Chapel of St. Joseph at St. Joseph Village of Chicago," 6.

[15] Franciscan Communities, 6.

subsequent action by Joseph, that cements our understanding of Joseph as a just and righteous man.

> It is a very precise moment, that of 'being raised from sleep,' in which St. Joseph, a 'just' man, who had already decided to put Mary away privily, not only to avoid condemnation of her, but so that no harm should come to the child, is transformed from repudiator to father, despite the fact that he has not yet lived with her. In fact, St. Joseph does not speak, does not react, but trusts and obeys the admonitoring angel, thereby becoming an instrument in the hands of God.[16]

The story of Joseph's dream is interwoven with another heavenly message, that of Mary's Annunciation. "He accepted as truth coming from God the very thing that she had already accepted at the annunciation."[17] Joseph, Pope John Paul II observes, "showed a readiness of will like Mary's with regard to what God asked of him through the angel."[18] This story paints a picture of St. Joseph ready and open to the unexpected movements of God's plans.

On the Feast of St. Joseph in 1961, as he and the Church prepared for the opening of the Second Vatican Council, Pope John XXIII issued *Le Voci.* In this apostolic letter, he reminds the reader that St. Joseph was the subject of the first two ideas presented to Pope Pius IX at the First Vatican Council, namely inserting his name into the sacred liturgy and proclaiming him the "Patron of the Universal Church."[19]

---

[16] Sandro Barbagallo, *St. Joseph in Art: Iconology and Iconography of the Redeemer's Silent Guardian* (Vatican City: Edizioni Musei Vaticani, 2014), 17.

[17] Pope John Paul II, *Redemptoris Custos: Apostolic Exhortation on the Person and Mission of Saint Joseph in the Life of Christ and of the Church,* August 15, 1989, Vatican.va, 4.

[18] Pope John Paul II, *Redemptoris Custos,* 3.

[19] Pope John XXIII, *Le Voci Che Da Tutti: For the Protection of St Joseph on the Second Vatican Council, March 19, 1961,* http://www.papalencyclicals.net/john23/j23levoci.htm, 1.

St. Joseph, Pope John XXIII declared, would be the patron of the upcoming Second Vatican Council, an event which we now know led to many unexpected outcomes that still reverberate today throughout the Church. In 1961, of course, this was only known in the mind and heart of God—and maybe St. Joseph.

> But the council is intended for all Christian people who are interested in that most perfect flow of grace. ...
>
> Therefore, everyone—clergy and laity, young and old from all over the world, of all classes, races, colors—is interested in the council, and if they identify a heavenly patron to implore that divine power from above in its preparation and development ... none of the celestial patrons can be better trusted than St. Joseph, august head of the Family of Nazareth and protector of the Holy Church.[20]

By writing this letter on the Feast of St. Joseph, Pope John XXIII hoped to inspire excitement and "an extraordinary revival of zeal, to a participation in a more intense, ardent, and continuing prayer" for the upcoming "extraordinary event."[21] It was to be an event watched over by St. Joseph, no stranger to the extraordinary and unexpected in his ordinary life.

---

[20] Pope John XXIII, *Le Voci Che Da Tutti*, 2-3.
[21] Pope John XXIII, *Le Voci Che Da Tutti*, 7.

From the Manual of Prayers for the Sisters of St. Joseph of Newark, 1961

Short Efficacious Novena to St. Joseph Composed by Reverend Louis Lallemant, S.J.

This Novena consists in turning to St. Joseph four times a day (it does not matter when or where) and honoring him in regard to four points:

1. His Fidelity to Grace. Think of this for a minute, thank God, and ask through St. Joseph to be faithful to Grace.
2. His Fidelity to the Interior Life. Think, thank God, and ask.
3. His Love of Our Blessed Lady. Think, thank God, and ask.
4. His Love for the Holy Child. Think, thank God, and ask.

Only one point is to be taken for each meditation.

Prayer for
Unexpected Moments

St. Joseph, inspire us to be open to the unexpected Spirit-filled moments of life. Pray with and for us, that we too may see the extraordinary possibilities hidden in the ordinariness of life. Thank you for the many ways you modeled acceptance and loving response to God's love. May we too respond to God's gifts with faith, gratitude, and loving action.

Amen

Chapter 3: Present of Presence

"We can imagine what Joseph must have been thinking."
~ Pope Francis

IN OUR culture, Christmas is often thought of as a holiday for children. Yes, we celebrate the birth of the Christ child, Emmanuel—an astonishing present when you stop to think about it, the presence of God with us, and God as one of us. But that central purpose and meaning can easily get lost in the hype and hullabaloo of Christmas as a commercial and cultural event.

Think about the rituals around Santa Claus, for example. Not only does Jolly Saint Nick have to travel around the entire world on a reindeer-driven flying sleigh, park on the roof and, one presumes, feed said reindeer, he then has to either squeeze into a dirty chimney with a bag full of presents or otherwise figure out another unobtrusive way to break into the house. After delivering the presents, quietly so as not to wake up the family, he also must remember to sample the cookies and milk left for him by expectant children before he does the whole thing in reverse, again and again. It's a lot of pressure if you think about it.

[Spoiler alert] The real pressure of course is on the parents. How to afford all those presents? How to hide them from inquisitive offspring during the days before Christmas? How to entice antsy and anticipatory little ones to go to bed early enough on Christmas Eve, so that the real work can begin. I am sure that more than one parent, assembling a doll house or bicycle, trying to follow instructions that made little sense to tired eyes, found themselves wishing the jolly man in the suit would just appear with the gifts already assembled, wrapped and ready to go. He could have all the milk and cookies his heart desired.

My Friend Joe

In my house, Santa Claus did not leave wrapped presents. Instead, an assortment of unwrapped Christmas surprises for each of the five Francois children would be left on display on a different piece of living room furniture, so that the intended recipient could find (and play with) them in the early hours of Christmas morning, without waking our parents. Mom and Dad would enjoy a well-deserved lie-in on Christmas morning, as we luxuriated in the bounty that Santa Claus had left for us—and sometimes gazed enviously upon what he left for one of our siblings instead.

At a reasonable hour, Mom and Dad would appear in their finest pajamas. The kids would sit on the floor with rapt attention while our parents opened, one at a time, the carefully *wrapped* presents they had left for each other under the tree. Looking back, this annual Christmas ritual—witnessing Mom and Dad expectantly open a present chosen and given with intention by their loved one—was one of my favorite holiday experiences. We, their children, were present to them in this moment, witnesses to their love and care for one another.

* * *

As I got older, I began to understand the meaning of Christmas as just that, care for the other. During my teenage years, my Mom worked at the county detention facility for a non-profit organization which provided resources and support to inmates to help them prepare for life after release. Each Christmas, inmates who participated in the organization's decision-making courses and other programs were eligible to sign up for the Toys for Tots program, as a way to give Christmas presents to their own children.

My mother coordinated the Toys for Tots program at the jail. As a Catholic high school student needing to earn service hours required for graduation, I helped. It was a big deal even going to the jail, let alone going inside, walking through the metal detector, being screened and escorted to my Mom's office. I mostly remember a lot of locked doors, endless buzzers, sterile hallways, and barbed wire.

I never interacted with the prisoners themselves. Instead, I helped Mom and her coworkers organize the donated toys, separating them into groups by age, gender, and category. Later, we would escort the family members—grandmother, mother, aunt, wife, sister, girlfriend, or sometimes a brother or uncle—into the jail's conference room where the toys were on display for them to pick out for the child, on behalf of the inmate.

These women, for they were mostly women, must also have gone through the same rigamarole to even get into the jail for this gift selection ritual. I remember it as a bittersweet experience. You could sense the responsibility they felt in picking out just the right toy for a child who would be without their mother or father on Christmas. They must have been filled with a mix of emotions—anger, joy, sorrow, hope, gratitude, despair. We would explain to the person picking out the gift that the inmate had earned this opportunity to give their child a gift for Christmas by participating in the non-profit's decision-making courses. That too was part of the present, their effort and commitment to a better life after their release. I remember more than once seeing a moist eye when we shared this news.

Parents and guardians sometimes face a lot of pressure at Christmas, in the midst of life's daily challenges. So too, did Joseph and Mary on that first Christmas. First there were the suspicious questions about the way Mary's pregnancy had come to be. Now here they were, away from home and their own support system, unable even to find a decent location for the blessed event to take place.

Nevertheless, Joseph was present with, to and for Mary and the little one. Joseph himself was a shelter of sorts for the moment of the vulnerable in-breaking of God into our human experience. One of the first Christmas presents was his presence, his love, and his care.

From the Tradition

The cast of characters present in the nativity scene comes to us mostly from the second chapter of Luke's Gospel. First, we are told that Jesus was not born at home in Nazareth but rather in Bethlehem. While embarking on such a journey so late during a pregnancy might not make a lot of sense, it happens to families the world over due to extenuating circumstances, such as those fleeing war or natural disaster or otherwise experiencing homelessness.

In this case, we are told that it is because Caesar Augustus declared that everyone should go to their own town to be enrolled in the census. Joseph, being from the house of David, had to take his very pregnant wife "to the city of David that is called Bethlehem." Unfortunately, when they finally got to Bethlehem, not only did Mary find herself about to give birth but there was no room for them in the inn. Jesus, newly born, was adorned in swaddling clothes and laid in a manger.

Mary, Joseph and the newborn Jesus were cut off from their support system. They did not have family or friends nearby to visit and welcome Jesus into the world. Luke does tell us, however, that local shepherds stopped by, tipped off by the message of an angel, "and found Mary and Joseph, and the infant lying in the manger."

Matthew's Gospel, also in chapter two, adds to the drama and extends the list of those present on the scene. Not only that, these illustrious visitors brought presents. Magi from the east, having seen the star of the "newborn King of the Jews" at its rising, arrived in Jerusalem seeking to pay their respects. King Herod, terribly troubled by this news, consults his experts to ascertain where the Messiah is foretold to be born. He asks the Magi to go to the place, Bethlehem, to "search diligently" for the child and then bring him word so that he too might see the child.

In Bethlehem, the Magi "saw the child with Mary his mother." Where was Joseph? Perhaps he was out on an important task to provide for his family? In any case, the Magi kneeled before the baby, "opened their treasures and offered him gifts of gold, frankincense, and myrrh." Perhaps their greatest gift, however, was safety and secrecy. After being warned about Herod in a dream, "they departed for their country by another way," rather than returning to Herod to alert him of their whereabouts.

We reenact the nativity scene each Christmas and decorate our homes with cribs and crèches. As a child, my favorite job was to help the Magi travel from room to room throughout the house, ensuring that they did not arrive at the manger until Epiphany. Yet Joseph, the reason the family was said to be in Bethlehem in the first place, usually gets little attention.

This is also true in art. Joseph is often relegated to the corners of the nativity scene. Sometimes he is even depicted asleep on the job, or like in Matthew's telling of the visit of the Magi, missing from the scene completely.

When Pope Francis visited the United States, he spoke with a group of men and women experiencing homelessness. He spoke to them of Joseph at the nativity.

> Joseph had to face some difficult situations in his life. One of them was the time when Mary was about to give birth, to have Jesus. ...
>
> The Bible is very clear about this: there was no room for them. I can imagine Joseph, with his wife about to have a child, with no shelter, no home, no place to stay. The Son of God came into this world as a homeless person. The Son of God knew what it was to start life without a roof over his head. We can imagine

what Joseph must have been thinking. ... Like Saint Joseph, you may ask: Why are we homeless, without a place to live? And those of us who do have a home, a roof over our heads, would also do well to ask: Why do these, our brothers and sisters, have no place to live? Why are these brothers and sisters of ours homeless?

Joseph's questions are timely even today; they accompany all those who throughout history have been, and are, homeless.[22]

Do you see what Pope Francis does here? Any consideration of the nativity involves an interplay with our imagination. It is inspired by scripture and tradition, but we are (re)telling the story. We can imagine who was present, and what presents they gave to the Christ child. Pope Francis, speaking to men and women who know in their bones what it is like to be without shelter, to be turned away from a safe place to sleep, invites their experience into the story. He draws a connection between the experience of Joseph and their experience. Moreover, he also calls to those of us who have never been afraid of how and where we will find a safe space to sleep to extend our care and concern to those who still have not found room at the inn.

Joseph's presence, and his present of care and concern for Mary and Jesus, is indeed timely, even today.

Prayer to St. Joseph by Pope Leo XIII[23]

To thee, O blessed Joseph, we have recourse in our affliction, and having implored the help of thy thrice holy Spouse, we now, with hearts filled with confidence, earnestly beg thee also to take us under thy protection. By that charity

---

[22] Pope Francis, *Visit to the Charitable Center.*
[23] Pope Leo XIII, *Quamquam Pluries: Encyclical on Devotion to St. Joseph,* August 15, 1889, Vatican.va.

wherewith thou wert united to the Immaculate Virgin Mother of God, and by that fatherly love with which thou didst cherish the Child Jesus, we beseech thee and we humbly pray that thou wilt look down with gracious eye upon that inheritance which Jesus Christ purchased by His blood, and wilt succor us in our need by thy power and strength.

Defend, O most watchful guardian of the Holy Family, the chosen off-spring of Jesus Christ. Keep from us, O most loving Father, all blight of error and corruption. Aid us from on high, most valiant defender, in this conflict with the powers of darkness. And even as of old thou didst rescue the Child Jesus from the peril of His life, so now defend God's Holy Church from the snares of the enemy and from all adversity. Shield us ever under thy patronage, that, following thine example and strengthened by thy help, we may live a holy life, die a happy death, and attain to everlasting bliss in Heaven. Amen.

Prayer for the Gift
of Presence

St Joseph, thank you for your gift of presence to Mary, Jesus, and all God's family. Give comfort to those who, this night, do not know where they will find safe shelter. Encourage mothers and fathers who struggle to provide for their children, especially those facing a lack of affordable housing or fleeing from violence and natural disasters. Inspire us to give the gift of our presence, as well as material support and resources, to those in need.

Amen

Chapter 4: Rise and Take Up the Child

"I consider St. Joseph the special patron of all those forced to leave their native lands because of war, hatred, persecution and poverty."
~ Pope Francis

ONE EXTREMELY warm September afternoon, I joined 400 other people, mostly Catholics, for the Catholic Day of Action for Immigrant Children in Newark, New Jersey. Cardinal Tobin, another Joseph, led the way as we marched from St. Mary's Church to the Federal Building, where the offices of Immigration and Customs Enforcement are located. "Today," Cardinal Tobin told the crowd, "I stand in solidarity with my brothers and sisters in Christ to decry the treatment of children who bear the trauma wrought by immigration enforcement raids, separation from their families and indeterminate detention."[24]

I had discerned participating in nonviolent direct action that might lead to arrest, as a group of us would block the intersection outside the Federal Building, forming a human cross while we prayed the Rosary. This is the first and only time, as of this writing, that I have risked arrest as part of my commitment to peace through justice.

My prayer and discernment centered on solidarity with those whose lives are at risk each day in our immigration crisis. It felt important, critical even, to take a stand on behalf of the little ones, the minor children who are detained and suffering on our border, many separated from their families.

---

[24] Sarah Salvadore, "Cardinal Tobin Leads Hundreds of Catholics in Protest Against ICE in Newark," *National Catholic Reporter,* September 6, 2019, http://www.ncronline.org/news/justice/cardinal-tobin-leads-hundreds-catholics-protest-against-ice-newark.

In the end, I was not arrested, although a few protesters were briefly taken into custody.

It turned out that my biggest challenge that day was the heat, which was close to 100 degrees. At one point, I felt weak and had to step away and take a seat on the sidewalk. A friend of mine noticed and encouraged me to move into the shade of a bus shelter while she went to get me some water and a snack. After just a few hours of walking and standing in the sun, I was already suffering from minor heat stroke. Imagine what the experience is like for those who walk hundreds or thousands of miles, through jungle and desert, seeking safety and the promise of a better life.

* * *

Around my neck I wore a picture of Juan de Leon Gutierrez, a young man from Guatemala who died in federal custody at the age of 16. For generations, Juan's family had been subsistence farmers, but an extensive multi-year drought meant his family's entire crop of maize and beans was lost. A story about Juan in *Time* magazine reports that he decided his only option was to migrate to the US to reunite with his 25-year-old brother who lived in Miami, so that he could send money home to the family.[25]

Juan left Guatemala on April 4, 2019. Just fifteen days later he was apprehended by US Border Patrol agents near El Paso, Texas. An unaccompanied minor, he was held in custody. A doctor noticed Juan was sick and sent him to the hospital. Juan had a brain infection, the cause of which was unknown—maybe a sinus infection, maybe head trauma. Juan died in federal custody on April 30. That day in Newark,

---

[25] Anna-Catherine Brigida, "He Went Seeking Life But Found Death: How a Guatemalan Teen Fleeing Climate Change Ended Up Dying in a U.S. Detention Center, *Time*, May 13, 2019, http://time.com/5587817/juan-de-leon-gutierrez-guatemala-migrant/.

I stood up for Juan's human dignity and the dignity of all minor children who face such dangers at the border.

While we were standing outside the Federal Building, a woman crossed the street with her grandchildren in tow. She was anxiously waiting for her daughter, the children's mother, who was inside the Federal Building, meeting with Immigration officials regarding a pending deportation order. Her daughter had been asked to bring her passport and a one-way ticket to Honduras.

The presence of the demonstrators outside the Federal Building moved her. She told us that her name was Angela Lopez and that we gave her strength, simply by being there. "I'm grateful to the United States, the Catholics that are here today and I'm going to keep fighting for my grandchildren," she said. She joined us in prayer, lying down on the street with the others who had formed a cross in the intersection as part of our peaceful protest, praying the Rosary.[26]

Angela told us that our presence made a difference. We were standing up for—and indeed lying down for—human dignity. We gave her strength, and she in turn gave us strength. That day, her daughter was our daughter. Her grandchildren were our grandchildren. She was our sister. It was a powerful example of mutuality and solidarity. We lived out of the reality that we have responsibility for each other, as members of one human family, with God-given dignity, no matter which side of the border we happened to be born on.

* * *

A few months earlier, I snapped the photograph of the Holy Family at St. Hugh's Church in Lincoln, England, while visiting the parish with some of our sisters and associates for the annual Nottingham Diocese Justice and Peace Day. I was

---

[26] Salvadore, "Cardinal Tobin Leads Hundreds of Catholics in Protest Against ICE in Newark."

drawn to this marble relief of Joseph, Mary, and the infant Jesus. I prayed for the intercession of the Holy Family for all holy families crossing borders or internally displaced today, seeking refuge, asylum, safety, and a better life.

Angela's determination that day, holding her arms around her grandchildren, reminds me of the look on Joseph's face, etched in marble. Here he is leading his family to safety; here she was protecting her grandchildren on behalf of her daughter. He pauses to look back and make sure Mary and Jesus are safe; Angela paused to join us in our nonviolent solidarity action.

Joseph and Mary knew what it felt like to have to drop everything and flee. They knew the precarious feeling of anxiety, not knowing what lay around the corner on their journey. They no doubt relied on the charity of strangers. Who would not risk all for their children, grandchildren, sisters, and brothers?

The foundation of our Christian faith, with Joseph leading his family, points the way.

> In a word, it is not only the cause of migrants at stake; it is not just about them, but about all of us, about the present and future of the human family. Migrants, especially those who are most vulnerable, help us to read the "signs of the times". Through them, the Lord is calling us to conversion, to be set free from exclusivity, indifference, and the throw-away culture. Through them, the Lord invites us to embrace fully our Christian life and to contribute, each according to his or her proper vocation, to the building up of a world that is more and more in accord with God's plan.[27]

---

[27] Pope Francis, *Message for the 105th World Day of Migrants and Refugees*, September 29, 2019, Vatican.va.

From the Tradition

The Holy Family's flight to Egypt is recorded in Matthew's Gospel. Shortly after the Magi's visit to the infant Jesus in the manger, an angel appears once again to Joseph in a dream. "Rise, take the child and his mother, flee to Egypt, and stay there until I tell you. Herod is going to search for the child to destroy him" (2:13). Promptly, Joseph acts on the message of the angel to protect his family, bundling them up and departing for Egypt under cover of night.

The next section of Matthew's Gospel paints the reality of the injustice they are fleeing—sadly an injustice that takes the lives of many innocents. At King Herod's order, all the male children under age two living in Bethlehem and the vicinity are murdered. It is not until after the death of Herod that the angel appears again in a dream to Joseph in Egypt: "Rise, take the child and his mother and go to the land of Israel, for those who sought the child's life are dead" (2:20).

* * *

In his 1952 Apostolic Constitution, *Exsul Familia Nazarethana,* Pope Pius XII declares the Holy Family as the "archetype of every refugee family."

> Jesus, Mary and Joseph, living in exile in Egypt to escape the fury of an evil king, are, for all times and all places, the models and protectors of every migrant, alien and refugee of whatever kind who, whether compelled by fear of persecution or by want, is forced to leave his native land, his beloved parents and relatives, his close friends, and to seek a foreign soil.[28]

This bold statement is not surprising when you put the pontificate of Pius XII in its historical context, beginning at

---

[28] Pope Pius XII, *Exsul Familia Nazarethana,* 1952, http://www.papalencyclicals.net/pius12/p12exsul.htm.

the start of World War II and crimes against humanity during the *Shoah,* the Nazi Holocaust.

> As it is well known, soon after we were raised to the See of Rome there daily appeared more bold and violent symptoms of unrestrained desire for extending national boundaries, for an idolized supremacy of rage and the unbridled tendency to occupy foreign lands, and for reliance on might rather than on right with the consequent cruel and shameless deportation of entire nations and the forced migration of peoples.[29]

In using the Holy Family as the foundation and model, he makes it clear that families have the right to migrate. Later Popes have also pointed to the example of the Holy Family, both to mobilize the church to charity and justice for migrants, and in pastoral care of migrants themselves.

Pope Benedict, for example, recognized the dignity of the Holy Family through their flight, similar to the "difficulties that every migrant family lives through, the hardships and humiliations, the deprivation and fragility of millions and millions of migrants, refugees and internally displaced people."[30] Pope Francis deepens this understanding, asserting that "Jesus, Mary and Joseph knew what it meant to leave their own country and become migrants."[31] In *Patris Corde,* Pope Francis writes: "I consider Saint Joseph the special patron of all those forced to leave their native lands because of war, hatred, persecution and poverty."[32]

To migrants and refugees themselves, Pope Francis wrote: "Do not lose your faith and hope! Let us think of the Holy Family during the flight in Egypt: Just as the maternal heart

---

[29] Pope Pius XII, *Exsul Familia Nazarethana.*

[30] Pope Benedict, *Message for the 93rd World Day of Migrants and Refugees 2007,* October 18, 2006, Vatican.va.

[31] Pope Francis, *Message for the World Day of Migrants and Refugees 2014,* August 5, 2014, Vatican.va.

[32] Pope Francis, *Patris Corde,* 5.

of the Blessed Virgin and the kind heart of Saint Joseph kept alive the confidence that God would never abandon them, so in you may the same hope in the Lord never be wanting."[33]

Prayer to St. Joseph by Pope Francis[34]

Father, you entrusted to Saint Joseph what you held most precious: the child Jesus and his Mother, in order to protect them from the dangers and threats of the wicked.

Grant that we may experience his protection and help. May he, who shared in the sufferings of those who flee from the hatred of the powerful, console and protect all our brothers and sisters driven by war, poverty and necessity to leave their homes and their lands to set out as refugees for safer places.

Help them, through the intercession of Saint Joseph, to find the strength to persevere, give them comfort in sorrows and courage amid their trials.

Grant to those who welcome them some of the tender love of this just and wise father, who loved Jesus as a true son and sustained Mary at every step of the way.

May he, who earned his bread by the work of his hands, watch over those who have seen everything in life taken away and obtain for them the dignity of a job and the serenity of a home.

We ask this through Jesus Christ, your Son, whom Saint Joseph saved by fleeing to Egypt, and trusting in the intercession of the Virgin Mary, whom he loved as a faithful husband in accordance with your will. Amen.

---

[33] Pope Francis, *Message for the 101st World Day of Migrants and Refugees 2015, September 3, 2014,* Vatican.va.

[34] Pope Francis, *Message for the 106th World Day of Migrants and Refugees 2020, September 27, 2020,* Vatican.va.

Prayer to St. Joseph, Refugee

St. Joseph, inspire your family to rise up, speak out, and care for migrants, refugees and asylum seekers today. May your example and the witness of the Holy Family provide comfort and inspiration to holy families crossing borders or internally displaced across the globe. Help us to stand in solidarity and work for just immigration laws. We ask your intercession especially for families who are separated and all immigrants in detention or awaiting deportation decisions.

Amen

Chapter 5: Limitless Family

"Son, why have you done this to us? Your father and I have been looking for you with great anxiety."
~ Luke 2:48

MY RELATIONSHIP with my father was complex, as I suspect are many father-child relationships, since time began. Maybe we were too alike. Perhaps we were too different. Could both be possible?

In childhood, of course, things were simpler. I have fond memories of Dad taking us on long drives in the car, singing Irish songs and honking the horn during the song's refrain, whenever there were no other cars nearby. Silly Dad was fun.

When I later entered the contrarian adolescent phase of my life, and my father's own career became more demanding, our father-daughter time was harder to come by and harder to bear—for both of us I suspect. Car rides were no longer the sound stage for impromptu singalongs, but rather became fraught with disagreement or very loud silence. Were you to ask me what we fought about then, I honestly cannot remember, other than that of course I was right and he was clearly wrong. Remember, I was a teenager and knew everything there was to know.

As the youngest of five children, I experienced a somewhat different family dynamic than my older siblings. One by one they went off to college, but I was still at home—until I wasn't. When I turned 18, I went to college 3,000 miles away and stayed there after college to begin my own career. While I spoke weekly with Mom and Dad and flew home for significant holidays, I also began to establish my own identity as a young adult in a new way, separate from my parents.

* * *

Flash forward about 10 years. My mother became very sick, first with cancer, then with a septic leg ulcer that led to amputation, and finally the return of the cancer with a vengeance. Over those long three years of illness, my Dad was faithfully at my Mom's side, every step of the way. He had recently retired, and his main occupation now became visiting Mom at the hospital or in the nursing home each day. When she was able to be at home, whether for a few days or weeks, he would take her to and from various medical appointments and make sure she was comfortable in between.

While each of their five children had left the nest and moved away from our Maryland home—to California, Chicago, Portland, and Europe—we made sure that Dad had company on his journey with Mom, most of the time, and whenever possible. One by one we took turns, putting our own lives on hold to be there with them. It was hard. It was wonderful. It was family personified, a sacred opportunity to return the unconditional love of our parents and to experience sibling solidarity and mutuality. As a bonus, we also got to spend quality time with Dad in the everyday moments of life in this extraordinary time—grocery shopping, laundry, and meal preparation.

* * *

After Mom's death, Dad was on his own, essentially for the first time ever. He faced his own health challenges and moved into an assisted living facility in Georgetown. I began to spend more and more time visiting him and discovered a new form of father-daughter relationship—presence. Eventually, Dad moved to a retirement community in Chicago to be closer to my sister and her family.

As it happened, my community missioned me to spend two years in Chicago for graduate theology studies. We set up regular father-daughter play dates on the days I did not have classes. Our time together became enjoyable again, in small doses, as I visited him in his assisted living apartment. Silly

Dad made regular appearances. We'd play games, watch movies, take naps, and go for drives. Rarely did our time together devolve into disagreement. Rather, I'd say it was characterized by gratitude, on both sides.

These visits continued, on a less frequent schedule, after I moved away to begin my new community ministry in New Jersey. Unfortunately, once the coronavirus pandemic hit, safety restrictions made in-person visits almost impossible. I did manage to visit him once for 15 minutes, about seven months into the pandemic. Later when he was on hospice and close to death, my sister Monica was able to spend some time with him in his room under compassionate care rules. For that we are very grateful. We know that we share these experiences of distance and separation with countless families during the pandemic.

* * *

For the last 15 years or so of Dad's life, our roles were reversed. I was now there to care for him. One day a few years ago, just before Thanksgiving, I cleared my schedule and flew to Chicago to be with Dad. He was seriously ill and had been admitted to the hospital. My sister, who had stayed with him overnight in a chair in his hospital room, was leaving for a previously planned trip to visit her husband's family for the holiday. It was my turn to be with Dad, until another sibling could free up time in their own schedule. We're at our best during a medical crisis.

I arrived at the hospital at sunrise. The facility is named after St. Joseph, and in front there is a statue of Joseph, standing with his arms around a young Jesus, about 9 or 10 years of age. Jesus is looking up at Joseph, with his hand on Joseph's hand. It is a reassuring pose, one that speaks of relationship, love, and trust. I'd walked past it many times before, as my Dad lived next door.

On this particular morning, however, the statue stopped me in my tracks. Joseph looks out toward Lake Michigan. As I stepped bleary-eyed out of the car at the hospital to take over Dad-duty from my sister, unsure of what Dad's prognosis was, I spied Joseph watching the sun rise with his son. The scene spoke volumes to me deep in my heart—of love and care, duty and responsibility, hope and promise.

I stopped in front of the hospital to pray, breathing in the blessings of the moment and asking for St. Joseph's presence with me in the days ahead, just as he had been present to Jesus and Mary. I prayed that I could be present to Dad and all that lay before us. Fortified by Joseph's comfort and assurance, I stepped through the hospital doors, ready for the next chapter of my father-daughter relationship, whatever it may hold.

From the Tradition

St. Joseph, foster father of Jesus, watches over us and protects us, according to tradition, just as he did for the child Jesus. For this reason, Pope Pius IX named Joseph the patron saint of the Universal Church in 1870.[35]

We do not know what their family dynamics were like, other than the few clues left in sparse references to the Holy Family in the Gospels. For instance, Luke tells us that after Joseph and Mary presented Jesus in the temple, "the child grew and became strong, filled with wisdom" (Luke 2:40), no doubt through the care and model of his parents.

Luke also tells the story of a 12-year-old Jesus who wandered off from his parents (Luke 2: 41-51). "After three days they found him in the temple, sitting in the midst of the teachers, listening to them and asking them questions." You can just imagine Mary and Joseph, simultaneously

---

[35] Sacred Congregation of Rites, *Quemadmodum Deus.*

exacerbated and relieved, when they finally found him there. Mary's worry causes her to ask her son if he knows how much anxiety he caused his father. "Why were you looking for me?" replies Jesus "Did you not know that I must be in my Father's house?" His response is an unusual mix of divine son of God and human son on the cusp of adolescence. Yet Jesus also must have realized he had caused his parents unnecessary concern, so he turned his back, for now, on the interesting theological debates and went home with his mom and dad, "obedient to them."

What was it like for Joseph, raising such a special child? Pope Leo XIII tells us his 1889 encyclical, *Quamquam Pluries,* that Joseph's dignity, holiness, and glory sprung directly from his relationships with Mary and Jesus. "He set himself to protect with a mighty love and a daily solicitude his spouse and the Divine Infant."[36] He stood with them through thick and thin. As the cultural head of household, he earned a living with his carpentry skills and provided for their needs.

* * *

The story of the Holy Family is alive and well today and will continue long into the future. For Christians, the Holy Family is our family. Pope Leo XIII asserts that this divine household "contained within its limits the scarce-born Church." Mary, mother of Jesus, is the mother of all Christians. Jesus Christ is our brother. And Joseph, our foster father, "the Blessed Patriarch looks upon the multitude of Christians who make up the Church as confided specially to his trust, this limitless family spread over the earth ... It is, then, natural and worthy that as the Blessed Joseph ministered to all the needs of the family at Nazareth and girt it about with his protection, he should now cover the cloak of

---

[36] Pope Leo XIII, *Quamquam Pluries,* 3.

his heavenly patronage and defend the Church of Jesus Christ."[37]

We are part of a limitless family. No matter our own experiences of family—nuclear, extended, or chosen—as Christians we are part of the family of God, a limitless family spread over the earth. And Joseph, who first was called to his role by the message of an angel, is there for us when we need him, ready to spread his cloak of mighty love around us, guiding us, comforting us, and protecting us as members of this limitless family of love.

From the Manual of Prayers for the Sisters of St. Joseph of Newark, 1961

O Glorious St. Joseph, chaste Spouse of Mary, our good Mother, and foster father of Jesus, our amiable Savior: humbly prostrate at your feet, we choose you anew for our good father, and beg you to receive us among the numbers of your privileged children. We thank you with our whole heart for having given us a place in this holy family, of which you are the protector and father. Burning with a desire of responding worthily to our holy vocation, we conjure you with the most filial confidence to obtain for us its spirit and virtues. Yes, great Saint, grant that, following your example, we may every day make new progress in humility, obedience, recollection, the spirit of poverty, and above all, in the love of Jesus and Mary. May we, like you, find our delight in serving this sweet Jesus in the person of His suffering members, as you had the happiness of serving Him in His own person. Deign to crown all your favors by obtaining for us the grace to die, like you, in the arms of Jesus and Mary, that we may go to share your happiness in the company of our beloved Sisters who have gone before us, and who await us near you in the heavenly country. Amen

---

[37] Pope Leo XIII, *Quamquam Pluries,* 3.

Prayer for Families

St. Joseph, pray for us, your limitless family, bound together in love. Be with all families in good times and bad. Take special care of families separated for whatever reason. Defend us from ourselves, from our growing pains and insecurities, our hurts and complex family dynamics. Share our joy at new life and the promise of tomorrow. Be our comfort in times of trouble, and our guide always. Teach us your way of mighty love for our human family and daily care for Earth, our common home. St. Joseph, husband of Mary and father of Jesus, pray for us.

Amen

Chapter 6: Watching the Workers

"Accompany us in times of prosperity when the opportunity is given for an honest enjoyment of the fruits of our labors; sustain us in our hours of sadness..."
~ Pope Pius XII

WHILE THERE is a lot we don't know for sure about the life of St. Joseph, scripture and tradition tell us pretty confidently that he provided for his family with the work of his hands as a carpenter. It is not uncommon to find statues, like this one, depicting St. Joseph the Worker, where he is holding close to his heart the tools of his trade.

This statue of St. Joseph stands behind Holy Name Medical Center, a hospital in Teaneck, New Jersey, founded in 1925 by the Sisters of St. Joseph of Peace and local doctors. Holy Name continues to provide quality care today. This particular scene caught my eye on a winter's day in January 2019, as I was walking to my car after a meeting at the hospital. My attention was drawn not so much by Joseph as by what just happened to be parked in the background that day—a carpenter's van. My initial caption for the photo was "St. Joseph checks out the competition." At the time, I found it to be ironic.

Every day, no matter what is parked in the background, this statue of St. Joseph watches over the hospital. He has an unobstructed view of the entrance to both the emergency room and the Sister Patricia Lynch Cancer Center. Not only does he watch over the hospital workers who provide compassionate care day in and day out, he also watches over the patients seeking care and the family members who entrust their loved ones to the hospital. He has witnessed a lot of sadness and joy over the years—lives lost, lives healed, and new lives coming into the world.

My Friend Joe

* * *

A little over a year after I took this photo, Northern New Jersey became the epicenter of the coronavirus pandemic. Suddenly, Joseph had a lot more to watch over. The parking lot that Joseph overlooks was soon filled with tents to provide a safe space for outdoor testing and screening. Ambulances drove past Joseph as they brought patients with advanced symptoms of COVID-19 to the emergency room. Families dropped loved ones off, unable to enter the hospital with them or even hold their hands as they faced this new and unknown virus. Essential workers, from doctors and nurses to security guards, housekeepers, and kitchen staff, faithfully and courageously arrived for their shifts each day, not sure what they would face in their personal protective equipment. Sadly, several hospital workers lost their own lives to the virus.

While I may have found it ironic when I snapped the photo of Joseph checking out his fellow carpenters, soon he had lots of construction work to oversee. In just 30 days, the construction and maintenance staff at Holy Name created 276 negative pressure rooms and 120 intensive care beds to accommodate the influx of patients.[38] Their creativity was astounding, especially given that supplies were very limited. Much of the materials they used was purchased at local hardware stores. The spaces they designed ingeniously protected both patients and caregivers. It was nothing short of a miracle, and all under the watchful eye of St. Joseph.

Our religious community continues to sponsor Holy Name Medical Center. As a member of our Leadership Team, one of my roles is as liaison to our sponsored ministries. All I could really offer during those days was my prayer and a commitment to stay up to date on the situation by calling the

---

[38] "Covid-19 Hospital Retrofit." Holy Name Medical Center, http://www.holyname.org/help/covid19-construction.aspx.

hotline set up by the hospital to provide regular updates on the fast-moving crisis for staff and board members. Dr. Ron White recorded the hotline updates. In addition to giving status reports on the numbers of patients being treated in the hospital with coronavirus, he also used the power of storytelling to paint a vivid picture of the heroic work by the hospital's caregivers, in all departments.

Each morning, as part of my prayer time, I would dial the phone number, anxious to hear how things were going. Each evening, I would do the same. In between I would hold all the patients, staff, and family members in my prayer. Often, I would think of that statue of St. Joseph the Worker, overlooking all the activity. It gave me comfort, knowing that he was on the job, watching over and protecting all involved, a worker praying for workers in their hour of need.

During those initial months of quarantine, the voice of Dr. White was a lifeline of sorts for me, offering honesty, humor, and hope amid the crisis. Isolated at home in the safety of my own pandemic bubble with the sisters, I nevertheless felt connected to the heroic efforts taking place just a few miles away at the hospital.

* * *

I couldn't help but reflect on our early sisters who, in 1890, answered the call to serve when a smallpox epidemic broke out in Passaic, New Jersey. They too worked tirelessly to provide compassionate care during trying circumstances. And they too did it all while carpenters hammered away adding space on the other end of the building—no doubt also under the watchful eye of St. Joseph. An account of the time says that when that epidemic ended, the sisters were exhausted, while the doctors, visitors, and undertaker marveled at their superhuman courage and greatness of heart that sustained them almost beyond human endurance.[39]

The Constitutions of the Sisters of St. Joseph of Peace say that Joseph's "courage to live a life of faith inspires us to trust in God's abiding love, especially in times of struggle and uncertainty" (Constitution 36). While scripture is light on the details of his daily struggles and work, our Christian story is testament to the fact that he faced uncertainty with courage and greatness of heart. "God acted by trusting in Joseph's creative courage," writes Pope Francis.[40] Who better to have standing over the comings and goings of the workers and patients at the hospital, watching out in good times and bad?

From the Tradition

The Gospel according to Matthew tells us directly, and early on, that Joseph was "a righteous man" (Matthew 1: 19). It's not until much later, however, when an adult Jesus faces his dubious home crowd in Nazareth, that we hear indirectly about Joseph's profession. Almost as an aside, his neighbors dismissal Jesus and his message by asking, "Is he not the carpenter's son?" (Matthew 13: 55). Mark's Gospel echoes the dismal, "Is he not the carpenter," (Mark 6:3), leaving out even the oblique reference to Joseph. There we have it—the length and breadth of the scriptural references to the work of Joseph.

These references, in particular the way the word carpenter is dropped as one snide remark among many, do not seem to make the case that it was considered to be a very dignified or noble profession, at least not in the recorded opinion of these naysayers. Yet tradition expands the biography and profession of Joseph so much that, in 1955, Pope Pius XII announced the creation of a new feast day to be celebrated on

---

[39] P.R. McCaffrey, *From Dusk to Dawn: A History of the Sisters of St. Joseph of Newark, New Jersey.* (New York: Benziger Brothers, 1932), 51.

[40] Pope Francis, *Patris Corde,* 4.

May 1st in honor of St. Joseph the Worker, "the humble craftsman of Nazareth," who personifies the "dignity of the worker."[41]

* * *

Human experience teaches us that a skill or trade is often passed down from parent to child. It is therefore not surprising that church tradition, informed by lived experience, fills in some of the details over time.

For example, texts such as the apocryphal Syriac Infancy Gospels, compiled as early as the sixth century, paint the picture of Jesus helping Joseph in his carpentry work.

> And Joseph used to go about through the whole city, and take the Lord Jesus with him, when people sent for him in the way of his trade to make for them doors, and milk-pails, and beds, and chests; and the Lord Jesus was with him wherever he went. As often, therefore, as Joseph had to make anything a cubit or a span longer or shorter, wider or narrower, the Lord Jesus stretched His hand towards it; and as soon as He did so, it became such as Joseph wished. Nor was it necessary for him to make anything with his own hand, for Joseph was not very skillful in carpentry.[42]

The passage is both practical and mystical, with references to doors, milk-pails and cubits and the awesome power of Jesus even as a child. It also is audacious enough, in order to stress the divinity of Jesus, to throw doubt on the actual human skills and craftsmanship of Joseph!

---

[41] Pope Pius X, "Prayer to St. Joseph the Worker," May 1, 1955, quoted in Philip Kosloski, "Begin your workday with this prayer to St. Joseph," Church, *Aleteia*, May 1, 2018, http://aleteia.org/2018/05/01/begin-your-workday-with-this-powerful-prayer-to-st-joseph-the-worker/.

[42] A. Cleveland Coxe, Alexander Roberts, and James Donaldson, eds., "The Arabic Gospel of the Infancy of the Saviour," in *Ante-Nicene Fathers*. New York: Christian Literature Publishing Co., 1886. http://gnosis.org/library/infarab.htm.

Fourteen centuries later in *Redemptoris Custos,* his apostolic exhortation on St. Joseph, Pope John Paul II claims that the scant references to Josephs' profession as a carpenter in the canonical Gospels are nevertheless enough to tell the whole story. "This simple word," *carpenter,* "sums up Joseph's entire life." He was a carpenter who raised his son to know the value and dignity of work. Jesus, "having learned the work of his presumed father," was known as "the carpenter's son."[43]

John Paul II teaches that through the institution of May 1st as the liturgical memorial of St. Joseph the Worker, the church recognizes the "special prominence" of human work, especially manual labor. "Along with the humanity of the Son of God, work too has been taken up in the mystery of the Incarnation, and has also been redeemed in a special way." Jesus, working alongside Joseph, "brought human work closer to the mystery of the Redemption."[44]

Prayer to St. Joseph, Model of Workers[45]

O Glorious Patriarch, St. Joseph, humble and just artisan of Nazareth, thou hast given to all Christians and particularly to us an example of a perfect life through diligent labor and admirable union with Jesus and Mary. Assist us in our daily work in order that we, Catholic artisans, may also see in it an effective means of glorifying God, of sanctifying ourselves, and of being a useful member in the society in which we live. These should be the highest ideals for all our actions.

O Dearest Protector, obtain for us from the Lord humility and simplicity of heart; love for our work and kindness toward our fellow-laborers; conformity to God's will in the unavoidable

---

[43] Pope John Paul II, *Redemptoris Custos,* 22.

[44] Pope John Paul II, *Redemptoris Custos,* 22.

[45] Pope Pius XII, "Prayer to St. Joseph, Model of Workers," quoted in "Let's Get to Work!" *The Divine Mercy,* May 1, 2019, http://www.thedivinemercy.org/articles/lets-get-work

trials of this life together with joy in bearing them; recognition of our specific social mission and a sense of responsibility; the spirit and discipline of prayer; docility and respectfulness toward superiors; the spirit of brotherhood [and sisterhood] towards our equals; charity and indulgence with our dependents.

Accompany us in times of prosperity when the opportunity is given for an honest enjoyment of the fruits of our labors; sustain us in our hours of sadness, when Heaven seems to be shut in our regard, and even the very tools with which our hands toil appear to rebel against us.

Grant that, in imitation of thee, we may keep our eyes fixed on our Mother, Mary, thy dearest Spouse, who, as she spun silently in the corner of thy shop, would let her sweetest smile course over her lips. Besides, may we never take our eyes off Jesus, who was busily occupied with thee at the carpenter's bench, in order that we in like manner may lead on earth a peaceful and holy life, a prelude to the life of eternal happiness that awaits us in Heaven forever and ever. Amen.

My Friend Joe

Prayer for Our Daily Work

Dear St. Joseph, you who used your skills as a carpenter to provide for your family, watch over and protect us. Inspire us to embrace the God-given gift of the co-creative power of work. Your humble example, barely recorded in the Gospels, is enough to help us understand the dignity of human work and workers. Be our companion in good times and bad. Help us to face the daily challenges, and the extraordinary ones too, even as we pause to spot glimpses of joy in our shared life. We pray that policy makers and employers will recognize and respect the rights of workers. Knowing that you passed along your knowledge to Jesus, we ask you to guide us in our daily work.

Amen

Chapter 7: A Happy Life

"The mystical implication is that this joy is not just inside [the human person] but surrounds [them] everywhere and absorbs [them]."
~ St. Bernard of Sienna [adapted]

WHY IS IT that we sometimes wait until the end of a loved one's life to have those real conversations? Not about comings and goings, this or that, but about life and love—real life, meaning, happiness, sorrows, questions, and true connections.

The lesson I am learning is, don't wait. The end may be expected. Time and circumstance may allow for the long put off heart-to-hearts to finally take place, but there is no guarantee.

Toward the expected end of my mother's far-too-long journey to life with God, I was able to have several of those moments. My last visit, about a month before she passed away, was filled with everything under the sun. I could tell that she was checking in to make sure that I would be okay when she was gone. We talked about God. She was certainly delighted that I had found my way back to the Church just a few years earlier, although I had not yet started to discern becoming a Catholic sister. Nevertheless, I think she knew this spiritual grounding would help me when she was gone. We talked about the state of the world, the war raging in Iraq, and the impact of government policies on people on the margins. I come by my interest in peace through justice naturally.

We also just held each other's hands and sat together quietly. Leaving that day, I knew it would be my last visit, and I was right. I had been preparing for my next trip to see her when I received the late-night call that she had passed away.

*　*　*

The other conversation etched in my memory, and on my heart, took place during one of Mom's earlier hospitalizations. It was my birthday, and I had made the trek from Oregon to Maryland to be with her, even if it meant we had to spend the day in the hospital. After all, our journey together on earth began in a hospital, with her labor and my birth, did it not?

What I remember most, less than anything we must have talked about, was the heart connection of mother and daughter. From her hospital bed, my mother was bound and determined that we would celebrate my birthday, and that meant cake. She sent me to the hospital cafeteria to find a slice of cake. No cake was to be found, however, and I returned with a sad little muffin. Mom clapped her hands and declared it my birthday muffin. Sharing that birthday muffin was better than any birthday party before or since. It was a eucharistic moment.

It was also a blazing hot day. That too is etched in my memory. When I left Mom to rest, I headed back to my car for a good cry before I drove home. First, as I'd been taught by none other than my mother, I reached to put on my seat belt. It was one of the old-fashioned varieties, with a metal clip on the end. While I had been inside with Mom, the seat belt had been soaking up the late July heat, and, when I grabbed the clip, it seared my hand. I remember holding onto the pain as a way of connecting with Mom's pain. I also knew that the stupid seat belt incident, as I now call it, would help me to remember that special hospital birthday and, of course, the birthday muffin.

*　*　*

We don't have details of Joseph's death, other than the tradition that it was a happy one. More on that later. Happy or not, I find myself wondering if it was expected or unexpected. I wonder how many of those heart-to-heart conversations Jesus and Mary were able to have with Joseph while he was still with them.

Did Joseph and Mary compare their angelic visits and tease Jesus about what would have happened if one or both of them had said no? I imagine the three of them gathered where Joseph slept, Mary perched on Joseph's bed, Jesus sitting on the floor, as they retold the story of their narrow escape on the flight to Egypt. Perhaps they shared their own version of the birthday muffin as they remembered the night in the manger and the gift of Jesus in their lives.

After Joseph died, did Mary hold in her hands a piece of wood he had carved, something he had touched and crafted? What memories were etched on her heart? For Joseph to have had a happy death, he must certainly have lived a happy life.

* * *

On one of my last visits with Sister Susan Dewitt, another dear loved one now gone home to God, I spotted the statue pictured at the beginning of this chapter in her room.[46] Her eyes lit up as she told me about this detailed wooden depiction of St. Joseph from the American Southwest. She encouraged me to get closer and to look at the little block of wood at his feet, and then at the bag of nails. She told me that there used to be miniature nails inside the bag, but they had gotten lost somewhere along the way. Or else, she conjectured with a laugh, maybe Joseph had just used them all up on his wood working projects.

As a carpenter, Joseph's life was no doubt productive. Perhaps at the end of his life, he reflected on how he had lived up to God's call to watch over and protect Mary and Jesus. He

---

[46] Susan Dewitt's book of poetry, *Traveling Empty: Poems*, was published by Kenmare Press in 2019.

could not be with them on the rest of their earthly journey, but he had done all he could while he was with them.

A happy life indeed.

From the Tradition

There is no description of Joseph's last days in scripture. In fact, there is no mention of Joseph at all in the Gospels after the incident where a twelve-year-old Jesus goes missing and Joseph and Mary find him in the temple. It is presumed that Joseph must have died between that event and the wedding feast at Cana, when Jesus attends the happy event alone with his mother. He was certainly not alive at the crucifixion, when Jesus entrusts his mother to his friend John.

While scripture is silent on his death, for centuries the faithful have understood St. Joseph to be the patron of the good or happy death. This tradition can be found in the writings of St. Irenaeus and St. Bernard of Sienna, though it has never been formally pronounced in the Catholic Church. Nevertheless, it is a presumed Christian theme, as evidenced in the ending prayer of Pope Leo XII's encyclical on St. Joseph: "Shield us ever under thy patronage, that, following thine example and strengthened by thy help, we may live a holy life, die a happy death, and attain to everlasting bliss in Heaven."[47]

* * *

A description of the death of Joseph is the subject of the *History of Joseph the Carpenter,* an apocryphal text from sixth or seventh century Byzantine Egypt. Written from the perspective, and in the voice, of Jesus, the text claims that Joseph died of natural causes, having never been sick before, at the ripe old age of 111 years. Fittingly, given the beginning

---

[47] Pope Leo XIII, *Quamquam Pluries.*

of the Christian story, an angel appeared to Joseph to foretell his death. Jesus, Mary, and other family members were with Joseph at his bedside during his last days. After his passing, the angels Michael and Gabriel took and "preserved his soul from the demons of darkness which were in the way, and praised God even until they conducted it into the dwelling-place of the pious."[48]

In the fifteenth century, St. Bernard of Sienna preached on Christ's love for Joseph and the joy of Joseph's life and afterlife.

> It is beyond doubt that Christ did not deny to Joseph in heaven that intimacy, respect, and high honor which he showed to him as to a father during his own human life, but rather completed and perfected it. Justifiably the words of the Lord should be applied to him, 'Enter into the joy of your Lord.' Although it is the joy of eternal happiness that comes into the heart of man, the Lord prefers to say to him 'enter into joy'. The mystical implication is that this joy is not just inside man, but surrounds him everywhere and absorbs him, as if he were plunged in an infinite abyss.[49]

While scripture may be silent, tradition is clear. Joseph lived a happy life and entered into joy in the afterlife, a good and happy death.

* * *

In the seventeenth century, this tradition flourished in Spain and the Americas. Charlene Villaseñor Black's research into the development of the cult of Joseph in the Spanish Empire leads her to observe that both written sources and artistic renderings of Joseph's death during this

---

[48] "History of Joseph the Carpenter," *Interfaith,* http://www.interfaith.org/christianity/apocrypha-joseph-the-carpenter, 23.
[49] Bernardine of Sienna. *Sermon 2, On St. Joseph.* Vatican website. https://www.vatican.va/spirit/documents/spirit_20010319_bernardino_en.html.

period have a "quotidian quality," expressing his passing as "commonplace, even humble, in nature."[50] His passing may have been humble, but in Spain and Latin America, St. Joseph's death, his *transitus,* was the subject of great ritual devotion by the people and many works of art. "Because these images were produced in an era of almost unparalleled mortality from disease, depictions of St. Joseph's death took on special poignancy by suggesting the heroic potential of ordinary suffering."[51]

Death and dying are undeniable parts of our human experience, which we continue to grapple with and try to understand. Joseph does not offer answers to perennial questions about suffering, but rather is himself an example of how to live joyfully and humbly, care for our loved ones and be cared for, and answer the call of God in the ordinary moments of life.

From the Manual of Prayers for the Sisters of St. Joseph of Newark, 1961

Prayer to St. Joseph for a Happy Death

O Blessed St. Joseph, who didst yield by last breath in the fond embrace of Jesus and Mary—when death shall close my career, come, holy father, with Jesus and Mary, to aid me, and obtain for me the only solace which I ask at that hour: to die under their protection.

Living and dying, into your sacred hands, Jesus, Mary and Joseph. I commend my soul.

Amen.

---

[50] Black, *Creating the Cult of St. Joseph*, 136-137
[51] Black, *Creating the Cult of St. Joseph*, 145.

Prayer for the
Living and the Dying

St. Joseph, help us to embrace life and to cherish every moment we have with our loved ones. You entered into life with joy fully as husband to Mary and father figure for Jesus. No wonder then that tradition tells us your death was equally good. We call on you Joseph to be with all who are dying, those who must say goodbye to their loved ones, all who are afraid of death, and all those who are alone in their final moments. In our sorrow, help us to hold onto the joyful moments, and to the promise that we will each be reunited in the love of God.

Amen

Conclusion: Your Friend Joe

Joseph is waiting in the wings, ready to answer our prayers. He desires to journey with us into the way of peace.

Growing up, one of my favorite book series was the *Choose Your Own Adventure* variety. The reader was invited to make choices which would lead to different story lines as they read the book.

Everyone's relationship with Joseph is different. Our life experiences lead us to lean on different aspects of Joseph at different times in our lives. In that spirit, I leave the writing of the conclusion of this book to you—to your experience, imagination, and prayer. Who is your friend Joe?

Here are a few prompts to guide your reflection:

Who is St. Joseph for you now?

What did you learn about St. Joseph that speaks most to your heart?

When do you go to Joseph? What big worries can you give over to his care?

Where have you seen St. Joseph in your life, whether an actual sighting of an artistic depiction, or in your own lived experience?

Why might you nurture your relationship with this just man and model of peace? How can you get to know St. Joseph better?

In closing, I repeat these words from the introduction:

My hope is that this book will help you to discover, or deepen, your own spiritual friendship with St. Joseph. ... However you read this book, my prayer is that you go to Joseph, and go in peace.

Appendix 1: Church Chronology on Joseph

1129	First church officially dedicated to St. Joseph in Bologna, Italy
1479	Feast of St. Joseph introduced by Pope Sixtus IV
1522	*Summa de donis sancti Joseph,* the first scholarly essay written on Josephine theology by Dominican Isidoro de Isolani
1555	St. Joseph named patron of New Spain by Provincial Mexican Council of the Catholic Church
1562	Discalced Carmelite Convent of St. Joseph founded by Teresa of Ávila in Spain
1621	Feast of St. Joseph made obligatory by Pope Gregory XV
1637	Novena celebrated in St. Joseph's honor in Puebla, Mexico, for his protection during storms
1650	Sisters of St. Joseph founded in Le Puy, France
1714	Proper Mass and Office for the Feast of St. Joseph confirmed by Pope Clement XI
1726	Inclusion of St. Joseph in Litany of the Saints ordered by Pope Benedict XIII
1870	Petitions presented to First Vatican Council asking that St. Joseph be declared Patron of the Universal Church
1870	St. Joseph declared Patron of the Universal Church by Pope Pius IX
1884	St. Joseph's Sisters of Peace founded in Nottingham, England
1889	Encyclical Letter on devotion to St. Joseph, *Quamquam Pluries,* issued by Pope Leo XIII
1909	Litany of St. Joseph approved by Pope Pius X
1920	*Motu Proprio* on St. Joseph and Labor issued by Pope Benedict XV

1921	"Blessed be St. Joseph, her most chaste spouse," is ordered to be inserted in the Divine Praises.
1922	Invocation of St. Joseph is ordered to be included in the special prayer at the moment of death.
1955	Feast of St. Joseph the Worker announced by Pope Pius XII
1961	St. Joseph selected patron of the Second Vatican Council by Pope John XXIII

Sources:

Barbagallo, Sandro. *St. Joseph in Art: Iconology and Iconography of the Redeemer's Silent Guardian.* Vatican City: Edizioni Musei Vaticani, 2014.

Black, Charlene Villaseñor. *Creating the Cult of St. Joseph: Art and Gender in the Spanish Empire.* Princeton, NJ: Princeton University Press, 2006.

Filas, Francis L. *Joseph: The Man Closest to Jesus: The Complete Life, Theology and Devotional History of St. Joseph.* Boston, MA: St. Paul Editions, 1962.

"Our History," Sisters of St. Joseph of Philadelphia. http://www.ssjphila.org/home/about-us/our-history/.

Teresa of Ávila. *The Life of Teresa of Jesus: The Autobiography of Teresa of Ávila.* Translated by E. Allison Peers. New York: Image Books, 1991. http://www.carmelitemonks.org/Vocation/teresa_life.pdf.

Appendix II: More Prayers to Joseph

Prayer to St. Joseph in times of anguish and difficulty

Glorious Patriarch Saint Joseph, whose power makes the impossible possible, come to my aid in these times of anguish and difficulty. Take under your protection the serious and troubling situations that I commend to you, that they may have a happy outcome. My beloved father, all my trust is in you. Let it not be said that I invoked you in vain, and since you can do everything with Jesus and Mary, show me that your goodness is as great as your power. Amen[52]

Prayer to St Joseph by Pope Francis[53]

Hail, Guardian of the Redeemer,
Spouse of the Blessed Virgin Mary.
To you God entrusted his only Son;
in you Mary placed her trust;
with you Christ became man.

Blessed Joseph, to us too,
show yourself a father
and guide us in the path of life.
Obtain for us grace, mercy and courage,
and defend us from every evil. Amen.

Memorare to St. Joseph[54]

Remember, O most pure Spouse of Mary, ever virgin, my loving protector St. Joseph, that never has it been heard that

---

[52] Prayer taken from a nineteenth-century French prayer book of the Congregation of the Sisters of St. Joseph of Mary. Included by Pope Francis in footnote 10 to *Patris Corde*. Pope Francis has prayed this prayer each day after Lauds for over 40 years.

[53] Pope Francis, *Patris Corde*.

[54] Sisters if St. Joseph of Newark, *Manual of Prayers for the Sisters of St. Joseph of Newark*, 1961.

anyone ever invoked thy protection or besought aid of thee without being consoled. In this confidence I come before thee, I fervently commend myself to thee. Despise not my prayer, O foster father of our Redeemer, but do thou in thy pity receive it. Amen.

St. Joseph, model and patron of those who love the Sacred Heart of Jesus, pray for us.

May the Divine assistance remain always with us.

May the souls of the faithful departed through the mercy of God rest in peace. Amen.

Novena for the Feast of St. Joseph (March 10 – 18)[55]

Litany of St. Joseph

Lord, have mercy on us.
Christ, have mercy on us.
Lord, have mercy on us.
Christ, hear us.
Christ, graciously hear us.

God the Father of heaven, have mercy on us.
God the son, Redeemer of the world, have mercy on us.
God the Holy Ghost, have mercy on us.
Holy Trinity, one God, have mercy on us.

Holy Mary, pray for us.
St. Joseph, pray for us.
Renowned offspring of David, pray for us.
Light of patriarchs, pray for us.
Spouse of the Mother of God, pray for us.
Chaste guardian of the Virgin, pray for us.
Foster father of the Son of God, pray for us.
Diligent protector of Christ, pray for us.

---

[55] Sisters of St. Joseph of Newark, *Manual of Prayers for the Sisters of St. Joseph of Newark.*

Head of the Holy Family, pray for us.
Joseph most just, pray for us.
Joseph most chaste, pray for us.
Joseph most prudent, pray for us.
Joseph most strong, pray for us.
Joseph most obedient, pray for us.
Joseph most faithful, pray for us.
Mirror of patience, pray for us.
Lover of poverty, pray for us.
Model of artisans, pray for us.
Glory of home life, pray for us.
Guardian of virgins, pray for us.
Pillar of families, pray for us.
Solace of the wretched, pray for us.
Hope of the sick, pray for us.
Patron of the dying, pray for us.
Terror of demons, pray for us.
Protector of holy Church, pray for us.

Lamb of God, Who takest away the sins of the world, spare us, O Lord.
Lamb of God, Who takest away the sins of the world, graciously hear us, O Lord.
Lamb of God, Who takes away the sins of the world, have mercy on us.

V: He made him lord of His household.
R: And ruler of all His possessions.

Let us pray.

O God, Who in Thine effable providence didst vouchsafe to choose blessed Joseph to be the Spouse of Thy most holy Mother; grant, we beseech Thee, that we may deserve to have for our intercessor in heaven him whom we venerate as our protector on earth. Who livest and reignest, world without end. Amen.

Devotion - Seven Sorrows and Joys of St. Joseph[56]

Our Father, Hail Mary, Glory Be (7 times) in honor of the Sorrows and Joys of St. Joseph

The Seven Sorrows of St. Joseph

1. The finding that his beloved Spouse had conceived, and the thought of his being obliged by law to forsake her.
2. His not being able to find shelter in Bethlehem for the Divine Child and His Virgin Mother except in a cold wintry grotto.
3. His seeing the Divine Babe suffer and shed His Blood at the Circumcisions.
4. His hearing at the Purification holy Simeon's prophecy that the Child would be contradicted and persecuted, and that a sword would pierce the Mother's heart.
5. His flight into Egypt with the Child and His Mother to save Him from the murderous fury of Herod.
6. His fear of Archelaus, Herod's successor, on returning from Egypt.
7. The loss of the Holy Child in Jerusalem, when for three days he and his holy Spouse sought the Divine Boy, sorrowing.

The Seven Joys of St. Joseph

1. His being reassured by the angel of Mary's innocence, and of the miraculous conception of the Holy Child.
2. The tidings of great joy brought by an angel to the shepherds, and the song of the angels.
3. The giving to the Child the holy Name of Jesus, as bidden by the angel.
4. The adoration of the newborn King by the three Wise Men.

---

[56] Sisters of St. Joseph of Newark, *Manual of Prayers for the Sisters of St. Joseph of Newark.*

5. The hearing from holy Simeon that the Child would be "the resurrection of many in Israel."

6. The hearing from an angel that he might safely return with the Child and His Mother from Egypt to the land of Israel.

7. The finding of Christ in the Temple after the three days' loss.

Prayer for the Feast of St. Joseph[57]

Preparation:

1. Create a sacred space that incorporates a statue, picture or icon of St. Joseph, and a candle.

2. Choose a song or chant to sing or listen to.

3. Choose a prayer leader and up to six readers (the prayer calls for six readers, but it can be adapted for fewer).

Introduction

Leader: As we gather to commemorate the festival of St. Joseph, our Patron, may we remember this person of peace with his special gifts of compassion, love, and trust as he cared for Mary and Jesus. May we have his wisdom and insight as we journey into the future.

(Sing a song or chant or play meditative music.)

Readings and Reflection:

Reader 1:

From the beginning of the congregation
Joseph was chosen as our patron
because he is a model of peace.
His courage to live a life of faith

---

[57] Sisters of St. Joseph of Peace, *Pray Peace: Prayers for Community Days and Celebrations* (Washington, DC: Sisters of St. Joseph of Peace, 2002), 21-23.

81

inspires us to trust in God's abiding love,
especially in times of struggle and uncertainty.
(Constitutions of the Sisters of St. Joseph of Peace)

Reader 2: Throughout his life, Joseph delighted in living constantly in God's presence. A righteous man, he was concerned for the things of God, he served and honoured God in trust, humility and obedience. Because of his attitude of heart and mind, Joseph was worthy to raise the Son of God in his own home. He gave Jesus knowledge, and practical wisdom, taught him to be steadfast and courageous—to be a man of faith, loving both God and neighbor.

Joseph stands as a model for Christians to emulate. Although not a martyr, he displayed a martyr's unswerving allegiance to his conscience and the word of God. He lived as a family man immersed in the world. He grew in peace and holiness by seeking to live in God's presence daily.

Reflective Pause

Reader 3: *Prayer of St. Francis*

Lord, make me an instrument of your peace;
where there is hatred let me sow your love;
where there is injury, pardon;
where there is doubt, faith;
where there is despair, hope;
where there is darkness, light;
where there is sadness, joy.
O Divine mater,
grant that I may not so much seek
to be consoled, as to console;
to be understood, as to understand;
to be loved, as to love;
for it is in giving that we receive;
it is in pardoning that we are pardoned;
it is in dying that we are born to eternal life.

Appendix II

Reflective Pause

Reader 4: Peace is a journey not an end in itself. We see this in Joseph's journey: in peace and uncertainty, but led by the spirit, he traveled the rough, uncertain roads to Bethlehem, to Egypt, to Nazareth ...

Reflective Pause

Reader 5:

> Personal prayer deepens our desire
> to be united with God in faith,
> enabling us to see God's presence and action in
> our lives and in the world.
> We commit ourselves to daily personal prayer.
>
> *(Constitutions of the Sisters of St. Joseph of Peace)*

Reflective Pause

Reader 6: "If we are peaceful, if we are happy, we can smile and everyone in our family, our entire society, will benefit from our peace."

(Thich Nhat Hanh, from *Peace is Every Step*)

Reflective Pause

Leader: Let us pray.

All: Give us faith gracious God when we cannot see clearly where our road through life is leading. In darkness and in doubt, may we always remember that you are near to hear the prayer of our hearts.

Reflective Pause

Intercessions

Have participants take turns in reading the prayers.

Loving God, you enabled Joseph to spend his life in your service. Set our minds on your kingdom and your justice before all other things. God in your mercy,

All: Hear our prayer.

Creator of the Universe, you have entrusted your work into our hands; grant that our labours may reflect your love and compassion. God in your mercy,

All: Hear our prayer.

Joseph, you took the child Jesus into your care, loving and accepting him as your own son. May we accept all that God gives us and care for those entrusted to us, especially the homeless, people living with AIDS and all those living on the margins of society. God in your mercy,

All: Hear our prayer.

Liberating God, free us with Joseph to rejoice with you over the goodness of your creation, make us heralds of the Good News and messengers of love and peace. God in your mercy,

All: Hear our prayer.

God of heaven and earth, by sending us your Son, Jesus, our brother, you have given us the opportunity to share in your divinity as you have shared in our humanity. May this holy exchange be the heart of all our celebrations. We make this prayer in Jesus' name, who is the Prince of Peace.

All: Amen.

Leader: Let us pray.

All: We thank you, St. Joseph, for your constant care and protection. As we journey on life's way, may we remain like you, strong in faith, firm in hope, active in charity. Help us to serve in liberty and peace. We ask this for ourselves and for all peoples through Jesus Christ, our brother. Amen.

Prayer Service for the Feast of St. Joseph[58]

Leader: Today we gather to reflect upon Joseph, patron of the Sisters of St. Joseph of Peace. Joseph was the son of Jacob, husband of Mary, parent of Jesus, a carpenter, and a dreamer. Scripture doesn't tell us much more about Joseph, and yet ....

> From the beginning of the congregation
> Joseph was chosen as our patron
> because he is a model of peace.
> His courage to live a life of faith
> inspires us to trust in God's abiding love,
> especially in times of struggle and uncertainty.
>
> *(Constitutions of the Sisters of St. Joseph of Peace)*

Let us spend some time with Joseph so that we may come to see how he can be a model of peace for us and our own work during our own times of struggle and uncertainty.

Getting to Know Joseph

Reader 1: *Discovery* by Sister Margaret Jane Kling, CSJP

> I journeyed within
> Searching for a symbol of justice
> That would speak to me of peace.

> And I found to my surprise,
> A refugee, a *campesino,*
> A person poor, simple and quite silent:
> One who dreamed dreams –and believed
> Who responded to the call—and hoped
> Who was led into darkness—and loved.

---

[58] Prayer service created by the author for Peace Ministries Inc., 2018, adapted from *Pray Peace: Prayers for Community Days and Celebration* and *125th Anniversary Reflection Booklet* (Sisters of St. Joseph of Peace). Pope Francis quotes are drawn from the Vatican website and news reports.

I found Joseph, called just
And the summons, live peace

Reader 2: Pope Francis also has a special relationship with Joseph. When he met with a group of men and women experiencing homelessness in Washington D.C. in 2015, Francis spoke with them about Joseph:

Reader 3: Joseph has been a support and an inspiration. He is the one I go to whenever I am "in a fix."

Reader 4: Joseph had to face some difficult situations in his life. ... Joseph was someone who asked questions.

Reader 5: But first and foremost, he was a man of faith. ... Faith sustained him amid the troubles of life.

Reader 6: As it did for Joseph, faith makes us open to the quiet presence of God at every moment of our lives, in every person and in every situation.

Quiet Reflection

- What are the areas of struggle and uncertainty you face in your life today? In your family? In your work? In community? In our world?
- How might you ask Joseph to journey with you/us at this time?

Litany of St. Joseph

Leader:
The following litany is inspired by the prayers of the Sisters of St. Joseph of Peace. Let us call upon Joseph to be with us on our journey.

[Participants take turn reading litany verse, all read response]

Joseph most just, prudent, and faithful ... Pray for us

Lover of people who are poor and on the margins ... Inspire us to work for a more just and compassionate world

Solace of the outcast ... Encourage us to welcome and respect all people

Model of peace ... Empower us to promote peace in our lives and ministry

Companion of displaced persons ... Awaken us to the needs of refugees and immigrants

Carpenter and artisan ... Guide us to work creatively for the common good

Hope of the sick and dying ... Inspire us to live compassionately

Patron of the Sisters of St. Joseph of Peace ... Lead us in the way of peace

Amen.

Prayer Intentions

Leader: We heard a few moments ago that Pope Francis goes to Joseph when he is in a fix. In fact, news reports have shared that he has a little statuette of Joseph at home. Beneath Joseph are little slips of paper where Pope Francis has written prayers for the troublesome situations he has entrusted to Joseph, the carpenter.

Reader 7: "You know, you have to be patient with these carpenters: they tell you they'll have a piece of furniture finished in a couple of weeks, and it ends up taking a month even. But they get the job done and they do it well! You just need to be patient." (Pope Francis)

Leader: *[pass out pieces of paper and pens]* I invite you now to spend a few moments in quiet reflection. Consider those areas where you might, like Pope Francis, "go to Joseph." What situations or concerns might you entrust to Joseph, model of peace? When you are ready, write your prayer intention on your slip of paper.

Closing Ritual

Leader: Good and gracious God, thank you for Joseph, an ordinary man of extraordinary love, justice and faith. Hear the prayers we hold for our world, work, and families. May our prayers be a source of light and empowerment as we call upon Joseph, model of peace, to journey with us. I invite you now to place your slip of paper under Joseph.

Let us pray:

All: Joseph, our patron and friend, be our guide as we walk in the ways of justice and peace. Teach us to be open to the surprising ways of God, to face the challenges before us together, to trust in our loving God, and to find beauty, wonder, and joy in the gifts of family and friends, creation and creativity, work and relaxation. Amen.

Bibliography

Barbagallo, Sandro. *St Joseph in Art: Iconology and Iconography of the Redeemer's Silent Guardian.* Vatican City: Edizioni Musei Vaticani, 2014.

Bernardine of Sienna. *Sermon 2, On St. Joseph.* Vatican website.https://www.vatican.va/spirit/documents/spirit_2 0010319_bernardino_en.html.

Black, Charlene Villaseñor. *Creating the Cult of St. Joseph: Art and Gender in the Spanish Empire.* Princeton, N.J: Princeton University Press, 2006.

Brigida, Anna-Catherine. "He Went Seeking Life But Found Death: How a Guatemalan Teen Fleeing Climate Change Ended Up Dying in a U.S. Detention Center." *Time,* May 13, 2019. http://time.com/5587817/juan-de-leon-gutierrez-guatemala-migrant/.

Congregation of the Sisters of St. Joseph of Peace. *Pray Peace: Prayers for Community Days and Celebrations.* Sisters of St. Joseph of Peace: Washington, D.C, 2002.

"Covid-19 Hospital Retrofit." Holy Name Medical Center. http://www.holyname.org/help/covid19-construction.aspx.

Coxe, A. Cleveland, Alexander Roberts, and James Donaldson, editors. "The Arabic Gospel of the Infancy of the Saviour." In *Ante-Nicene Fathers: The Twelve Patriarchs, Excerpts and Epistles, The Clementina, Apocrypha, Decretals, Memoirs of Edessa and Syriac Documents, Remains of the First Ages.* New York: Christian Literature Publishing Co., 1886. http://gnosis.org/library/infarab.htm.

Cusack, Margaret Anna (Mother Clare), "St. Joseph's Confraternity of Peace." 1883. Quoted in Joan Ward, CSJP and Catherine O'Connor, CSJP, *A Great Love of Peace: Insights into the Charism and Spirituality of the Sisters of St. Joseph of Peace* (Self-published, 2000).

Cusack, Mary Francis Clare. *Cloister Songs and Hymns for Children.* London: Burns and Co., 1881.

Day, Dorothy

"Day After Day," *The Catholic Worker*, October 1936, 4.

"May Day," *The Catholic Worker*, May 1956, 2.

Del Guercio, Gelsomino. "Why is Pope Francis so devoted to St. Joseph Sleeping and to the Virgin Mary, Untier of Knots?" Church, *Aleteia,* May 2, 2018. http://aleteia.org/2018/05/02/why-is-pope-francis-so-devoted-to-st-joseph-asleep-and-to-the-virgin-mary-untier-of-knots/.

Dewitt, Susan. "History and Roots: Reclaiming Peace." *Living Peace*, Winter 2014, 20.

Franciscan Communities. "Chapel of St. Joseph at St. Joseph Village of Chicago."

"History of St. Joseph the Carpenter." *Interfaith.* http://www.interfaith.org/christianity/apocrypha-joseph-the-carpenter.

McCaffrey, P.R. *From Dusk to Dawn: A History of the Sisters of St. Joseph of Newark, New Jersey.* New York: Benziger Brothers, 1932.

Pope Benedict. *Message for the 93rd World Day of Migrants and Refugees 2007.* October 18, 2006. Vatican website. http://www.vatican.va/content/benedict-xvi/en/messages/migration/documents/hf_ben-xvi_mes_20061018_world-migrants-day.html.

Bibliography

Pope Francis

Message for the 101st World Day of Migrants and Refugees 2015. Vatican website. September 3, 2014. http://www.vatican.va/content/francesco/en/messages/migration/documents/papa-francesco_20140903_world-migrants-day-2015.html.

Message for the 105th World Day of Migrants and Refugees 2019. Vatican website. September 29, 2019. http://www.vatican.va/content/francesco/en/messages/migration/documents/papa-francesco_20190527_world-migrants-day-2019.html.

Message for the 106th World Day of Migrants and Refugees 2020. Vatican website. September 27, 2020. http://www.vatican.va/content/francesco/en/messages/migration/documents/papa-francesco_20200513_world-migrants-day-2020.html.

Message for the World Day of Migrants and Refugees 2014. Vatican website. August 5, 2014. http://www.vatican.va/content/francesco/en/messages/migration/documents/papa-francesco_20130805_world-migrants-day.html.

Patris Corde: Apostolic Letter on the 150th Anniversary of the Proclamation of Saint Joseph as Patron of the Universal Church. Vatican website. December 8, 2020. http://www.vatican.va/content/francesco/en/apost_letters/documents/papa-francesco-lettera-ap_20201208_patris-corde.html.

"Visit to the Charitable Center of St. Patrick Parish and Meeting with the Homeless." Vatican website. September 24, 2015. http://www.vatican.va/content/francesco/en/speeches/2015/september/documents/papa-francesco_20150924_usa-centro-caritativo.html.

Pope John XXIII. *Le Voci Che Da Tutti: For the Protection of St Joseph on the Second Vatican Council.* March 19, 1961. http://www.papalencyclicals.net/john23/j23levoci.htm.

Pope John Paul II. *Redemptoris Custos: Apostolic Exhortation on the Person and Mission of Saint Joseph in the Life of Christ and of the Church.* Vatican website. August 15, 1989. http://www.vatican.va/content/john-paul-ii/en/apost_exhortations/documents/hf_jp-ii_exh_15081989_redemptoris-custos.html.

Pope Leo XIII. *Quamquam Pluries: Encycical on Devotion to St. Joseph.* Vatican website. August 15, 1889. http://w2.vatican.va/content/leo-xiii/en/encyclicals/documents/hf_l-xiii_enc_15081889_quamquam-pluries.html.

Pope Pius X. "Prayer to St. Joseph the Worker." May 1, 1955. Quoted in Philip Kosloski, "Begin your workday with this prayer to St. Joseph," Church, *Aleteia*, May 1, 2018. http://aleteia.org/2018/05/01/begin-your-workday-with-this-powerful-prayer-to-st-joseph-the-worker/.

Pope Pius XII

    Exsul Familia Nazarethana. August 1, 1952. http://www.papalencyclicals.net/pius12/p12exsul.htm.

    "Prayer to St. Joseph, Model of Workers." Quoted in "Let's Get to Work!" *The Divine Mercy*, May 1, 2019. https://www.thedivinemercy.org/articles/lets-get-work.

Sacred Congregation of Rites. *Quemadmodum Deus.* December 8, 1870. http://osjusa.org/st-joseph/magisterium/quemadmodum-deus/.

Bibliography

Salvadore, Sarah. "Cardinal Tobin leads hundreds of Catholics in protest against ICE in Newark." *National Catholic Reporter,* September 6, 2019. http://www.ncronline.org/news/justice/cardinal-tobin-leads-hundreds-catholics-protest-against-ice-newark.

Sisters of St. Joseph of Newark. *Manual of Prayers.* 1961.

Teresa of Ávila, *The Life of Teresa of Jesus: The Autobiography of Teresa of Ávila.* Translated by E. Allison Peers. New York: Image Books, 1991. http://www.carmelitemonks.org/Vocation/teresa_life.pdf.

Vidulich, Dorothy A. *Peace Pays a Price: A Study of Margaret Anna Cusack, the Nun of Kenmare.* Englewood Cliffs, NJ: Kenmare Press, 2019.

About Kenmare Press

Kenmare Press is an imprint of the Sisters of St. Joseph of Peace. In accord with our tradition and the spirit of our founder, Margaret Anna Cusack (Mother Francis Clare), we launched this publishing project in 2019, our 135th anniversary year. Mother Clare was herself a prolific writer, most often publishing as M.F. Cusack or Mary Francis Cusack. By 1870, more than 200,000 copies of her works had circulated throughout the world. Profits from the sale of her books were used for the sisters' work with the poor. Today, many of her books are in the public domain and available to read or download online.

In addition to *My Friend Joe: Reflections on St. Joseph*, we have published three books written by sisters that are available in paperback and eBook format at online booksellers and at csjp.org.

Peace Pays a Price: A Study of Margaret Anna Cusack by Dorothy Vidulich, CSJP

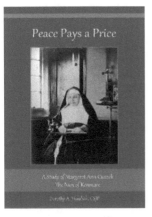

Margaret Anna Cusack was bold, courageous and visionary. She dedicated her life to fighting social injustice, especially toward the poor and woman and children.

Based on Cusack's many books, biographies, letters and other research, Sister Dorothy Vidulich has written a concise study of Cusack's life. In particular, she has focused on Cusack's courage to confront the discrimination and injustice promulgated by society and a patriarchal church, which ultimately forced her to leave the religious order she had founded for it to be saved.

The Sparrow Finds Her Home: A Journey to Find the True Self
by Doris J. Mical, CSJP

Sister Doris Mical reflects on how the people, experiences, and events in her life have directly impacted the spiritual journey that ultimately led her to find her true self.

Traveling Empty – Poems
by Susan Dewitt, CSJP

This collection of poems from Sister Susan Dewitt invites the reader on a holy journey through kitchens and gardens, women's shelters and desert retreat centers and beyond.

My Aunt Is A Nun

My Aunt Is A Nun is a podcast that features Sisters of St. Joseph of Peace sharing intimate accounts of their personal journeys. These rich and often surprising stories draw from thousands of years of religious heritage. They shed new light on the way spiritual perspectives can inform culture on love, leadership, politics, and our overall place in the world by bringing age old wisdom into modern sensibility. Join Megan Bell as she sits down with her aunt, a Catholic nun and former Congregation Leader, and other sisters to make pancakes, watch Netflix, tweet, sit in stillness, and sing to songbirds. The veils are off as they explore everything from anxiety to intimacy, prayer to politics, and poverty to justice. You can find *My Aunt Is A Nun* at myauntisanun.com and Apple Podcasts.